MONAGHAN

A Life

MONAGHAN

A Life

JOSEPH PEARCE

TAN Books
Charlotte, North Carolina

Cover Design: David Ferris, www.DavidFerrisDesign.com

Cover Image of Tom Monaghan: Dave Neill, DNG Naples Studio, used with permission. Cover Image of Joseph Pearce: Chris Pelicano, used with permission. Interior photos: Tom Monaghan personal collection, used with permission.

ISBN: 978-1-5051-0890-3

Published in the United States by
TAN Books
P. O. Box 410487
Charlotte, NC 28241
www.TANBooks.com

Printed in the United States of America

For Diane Eriksen

We are all in the gutter, but some of us are looking at the stars.

Oscar Wilde

CONTENTS

AUTHOR'S NOTE

I N THE writing of this volume, I have been blessed with an abundance of materials supplied by Mr. Monaghan, including a number of unpublished biographical manuscripts, as well as the transcripts of interviews. These, in addition to my own interviews with Mr. Monaghan and occasional quotes from James Leonard's interviews with him, form the foundation upon which the following edifice is built.

THE VIEW FROM THE GUTTER

WHEN I was initially commissioned by Tom Monaghan to write his biography, I will confess that I had severe misgivings. As someone who had been on the faculty of Ave Maria College from 2001 until 2004 and then on the faculty of Ave Maria University from 2004 until 2012, I felt that I was, at one and the same time, too close to the subject and yet also too far from it.

On the one hand, I owe a great personal debt of gratitude to Mr. Monaghan. If he had not started Ave Maria College, I might never have come to the United States. I might still be in my native land, an impoverished writer eking out a meager living in England's green but infertile land. On the other hand, I experienced firsthand the growing pains at the college and university and saw many of my friends become embittered toward Mr. Monaghan as he made decisions with which they disagreed vehemently. Even today, as the dust settles on those old disputes, I suspect that some of my friends will be angered by my decision to write what will be, for the most part, a positive portrayal of a remarkable man.

Any doubts that I might have had about writing the book were assuaged considerably after I picked up a copy of James Leonard's *Living the Faith: A Life of Tom Monaghan*.* While Leonard extensively documents Tom's life and conducted extensive interviews with Tom and others, interviews I have made use of here, his biography is marred by a fatal flaw: a scorn for his subject and an antipathy to the Catholic faith.

Throughout its almost four hundred sprawling pages, the author makes little or no effort to either sympathize or empathize with his subject, preferring instead to sit in supercilious judgment, passing sentence on every aspect of Tom Monaghan's life and beliefs. As I read this biography, I was appalled by the pride and prejudice of the author and by the catalogue of errors that protruded with irritating regularity from its pages.

Although Leonard was raised as a Catholic and educated at Catholic schools from kindergarten through high school, he lost whatever faith he had shortly after graduation. "I left the Church after I graduated," Leonard writes in the preface to his book, "went back after I got married, and left for good when I got divorced." After his lapse from the practice of the Faith, he claims to have read the Bible a few times, as well as the works of the Church Fathers and the Gnostic scriptures, before proceeding to read "the founding documents of most of the rest of the world's religions, and several shelves of books on religion after that" (xii). These

---

* James Leonard, *Living the Faith: A Life of Tom Monaghan* (Ann Arbor: University of Michigan, 2012).

facts are presumably given to the reader to establish Leonard's credentials, to let us know that he knows what he's talking about. Unfortunately, however, his book proves all too embarrassingly that he doesn't. On the very first page, he misquotes the words of the "Hail Mary." In the pages that follow, he displays again and again, as others have noted, a misunderstanding of Catholic belief and practice and hostility toward Catholicism and conservatism.

Why, one might ask, have I spent time criticizing a previous biography of Tom Monaghan as a means of raising the curtain on my own? It is simply that Leonard's debacle of a book served to energize my own labors. If I hadn't read his book, I would not have proceeded with the writing of mine with such a sense of passion and purpose. Few people have done more to shape the Church in the United States in the past thirty years than Tom Monaghan, and his contributions demand and deserve to be evaluated by a biographer who doesn't look upon the Faith from a perspective of ignorance and hostility. Tom Monaghan, for all his faults, does not deserve to be treated the way that Leonard treats him. This being so, Leonard's must not be the last word on the subject.

It's not that I intend to counter Leonard by writing a hagiography that depicts the pizza-billionaire-turned-philanthropist as a saint, so squeaky-clean that he needs oiling! On the contrary, I made it clear to Mr. Monaghan that I was not interested in writing such a book, and for his part, he made it clear to me that this was not the sort of book that he desired to be written. With this in mind, I am reminded of Raymond Arroyo's introduction to his biography of Mother Angelica, founder of the Eternal Word Television Network (EWTN). Although Arroyo was an employee of EWTN as well as one of Mother Angelica's closest friends and confidants, Mother was at pains that their relationship should not cloud Arroyo's judgment of her flaws and weaknesses. Here's the relevant passage from Arroyo's introduction:

> One evening, before shooting her live show, she gave me but one instruction, which has haunted me to this day: "Make sure you present the real me. There is nothing worse than a book that sugarcoats the truth and ducks the humanity of the person. I wish you forty years in purgatory if you do that!"
>
> Hoping to steer clear of that ignoble end, I have written a book that does not avoid controversy or the seeming contradictions inherent in Mother Angelica's character: the cloistered, contemplative nun who speaks to the world; the independent rule breaker who is derided as a "rigid conservative"; the wisecracking comedian who suffers near constant pain; the Poor Clare nun who runs a multimillion-dollar corporation.[*]

Although I have taken Arroyo's approach in his writing of Mother Angelica's biography as my own model and

---

[*] Raymond Arroyo, *Mother Angelica: The Remarkable Story of a Nun, Her Nerve, and a Network of Miracles* (New York: Image, 2007), xxi.

inspiration, I could certainly not claim to be one of Tom Monaghan's closest friends and confidants. Far from it. We are, at best, friendly acquaintances. He was a part of my life as the founder and principal benefactor of the institution at which I taught for eleven years. We met rarely and, when we did, usually only exchanged a few friendly and largely platitudinous words. There were times when his actions irritated me and times when his decisions angered me; and yet, as I've noted already, I will always be grateful to him for having opened up the huge vista of my new life in the United States, a *vita nuova* that might never have happened if he hadn't founded Ave Maria College, later to metamorphose into Ave Maria University.

There are, however, parallels between my position as Tom Monaghan's biographer and Raymond Arroyo's position as the biographer of Mother Angelica. Though we both had a business relationship with our subject, we were both intent on preventing that fact from clouding our view and our judgment, and we were both aware that our subject did not want sugarcoating and desired honesty. Like Raymond Arroyo, I have written a book that does not avoid controversy or the seeming contradictions inherent in my subject's character: the quiet, somewhat shy and introverted man who founded and owned Domino's Pizza and who bought the Detroit Tigers; the independent innovator who is derided as a "rigid conservative"; the ascetic pursuer of the simple life who was notorious for splurge-spending on fast cars, airplanes, and boats; the billionaire who desires to give his fortune away.

Like Mother Angelica, Tom Monaghan is an enigma whose life is a string of paradoxes. This being so, the following pages will seek to understand the enigma and to solve the riddles that his life poses. In order to do so, we have to move beyond the view from the faithless and materialist gutter that James Leonard's disfigured portrait presents. We need to see Tom Monaghan through his own eyes, to understand him as he understands himself; only then can we step back and make an objective judgment about the man and his life; only when we have plucked the plank of pride and prejudice from our own eye can we dare to see the mote in the eye of the other.

Like the rest of us, Tom Monaghan is in the gutter. He is a sinner and is prone to the weaknesses that plague sinful men. Yet, unlike the materialist or the seeker after self-gratification, he is not facedown in the gutter, believing that there is nothing but the squalor in which he finds himself. Living up to the noble Greek vision of man as one who looks upward (*anthropos*), Monaghan seeks for the meaning of life in that which is beyond his own egocentric "self," gazing beyond the gutter to the stars and to the God who made the stars. Since this is so, I can think of no better way to end the prologue to this book than the way in which I ended the preface to my biography of Oscar Wilde: " 'We are all in the gutter,' says Lord Darlington in *Lady Windermere's Fan*, 'but some of us are looking at the stars.' To look for Wilde in the gutter, whether to wallow with him in the mire or to point the finger of self-righteous scorn, is to miss the point. Those wishing a deeper understanding of this most enigmatic of men should not look *at* him in the gutter but *with* him at the stars."

Monaghan is very different in oh so many ways from Oscar Wilde, for better or worse, but he shares with Wilde this same vision of the stars and the same desire for the God who made the stars and for whom the stars are a mere metaphor.

Wilde ended his life as a Catholic, hoping thereby to get to heaven; Monaghan hopes, by the grace of God, to do the same. It is this hope that inspires him in all that he does. This is why, if we wish to see beyond the surface of Tom Monaghan's life to the core of his being and the depths of his heart, we need to understand that his own heart marches to the beat of the Sacred Heart that gives it life. This is why, if we want to understand the real Tom Monaghan, we will need to see beyond the gutter to the stars.

CHAPTER 1

A BIRTHDAY PRESENT

The test of all happiness is gratitude; and I felt grateful, though I hardly knew to whom. Children are grateful when Santa Claus puts in their stockings gifts of toys or sweets. Could I not be grateful to Santa Claus when he put in my stockings the gift of two miraculous legs? We thank people for birthday presents of cigars and slippers. Can I thank no one for the birthday present of birth?

G. K. Chesterton

THE MORE things change, the more they remain the same . . .

The world into which Thomas Stephen Monaghan was born, on March 25, 1937, was not that different from the world in which we find ourselves today. There were wars in various parts of the world, governments were becoming bigger and more powerful, and the traditional family and the traditional understanding of marriage were under attack. Franklin D. Roosevelt's New Deal was in full swing, dramatically increasing the role of the Federal Government in the economy and, in consequence, greatly increasing the power of central government over the lives of ordinary people. This trend toward big government was also *en vogue*, or perhaps we should say "all the rage," in other parts of the world. Fascism was fashionable, and so was communism. Mussolini was in power in Italy, and Hitler in Germany; in the Soviet Union, Josef Stalin ruled with an iron fist, crushing his own people with the power of his paranoia. This nightmare scenario, in which governments were getting too big for their jackboots, would inspire George Orwell, a few years later, to write his cautionary book about the evils of Big Brother.

As for the specter of war, it was looming large in March 1937. Japan was in the process of conquering China, and before the year was out, its soldiers would commit what has become known to history as the Nanking Massacre or the Rape of Nanking, in which as many as three hundred thousand Chinese civilians—men, women, and children—were slaughtered in cold blood, with many of the women first being gang-raped. In Spain, General Franco's Nationalist forces were in the ascendant, their offensive at Guadalajara on March 20 forcing the communist forces into retreat.

In the Soviet Union, the Great Purge, as it became known, led to the arrest on trumped-up charges of at least 1.5 million people in 1937 and 1938, of which almost half were summarily executed, a rate of one thousand executions a day. Meanwhile, in the Third Reich, the Nazi government began to forcibly sterilize nonwhite children as part of a program of racial purification inspired by the rise of the eugenics movement, which was growing in popularity worldwide, not least in the United States, where Margaret Sanger, as a leading member of the American Eugenics Society and a founding member of the American Birth Control League—forerunner of Planned Parenthood—preached and sought to practice the same sort of racial purification programs as those practiced by the Nazis. As editor of *Birth Control Review*, Sanger published headlines such as "More Children for the Fit. Less for the Unfit." As for whom she considered to be the unfit, she was happy to proclaim it from the housetops with brazen chutzpah: "Hebrews, Slavs, Catholics, and Negroes." She deliberately set up her first birth control clinics in immigrant neighborhoods and openly advocated that those considered "unfit" should be made to apply to the government for permission to have children "as immigrants have to apply for visas." Considering Sanger's position, it is not surprising that Nazi scientists from Germany were invited to publish articles in the *Birth Control Review* that she edited, nor that members of Sanger's American Birth Control League visited Nazi Germany and sat in on sessions of the Supreme Eugenics Court, returning to the United States with glowing reports of how the "Sterilization Law" was "weeding out the worst strains in the Germanic stock in a scientific and truly humanitarian way."

If this sounds shocking, it is even more shocking that one of Sanger's closest allies, C. C. Little, was on the cover of *Time*, smiling broadly and looking dashingly debonair, on the very day that Tom Monaghan was born. Little was president of the American Eugenics Society and cofounder, with Sanger and Lothrop Stoddard, of the American Birth

Control League. As president of the University of Michigan, he had proved controversial for his outspoken support for eugenics, birth control, and euthanasia. Much of his research was financed with grants from the big Detroit car manufacturers, in much the same way as the early eugenics and birth control movement had been financed by magnates such as the Rockefellers and the Carnegies. C. C. Little ended his days as an official spokesman for the Tobacco Industry Research Committee, doing his masters' bidding by claiming that smoking had no connection to cancer.

Those seeking other striking parallels between the world in which Tom Monaghan was born and the world in which we find ourselves today need look no further than the way in which some Christian churches were aiding and abetting the destruction of the traditional family in their support for the eugenics and birth control movement, thereby removing procreation, and openness to life, from marriage with all the inexorably destructive ramifications that have played themselves out down to our own day. Within a few weeks of Monaghan's birth, the Federal Council of Churches of Christ approved birth control, following the example of the Anglican Church, which had also given its blessing to birth control at its Lambeth Conference seven years earlier. As history has so tragically demonstrated, this embrace of the culture of death by liberal Christian denominations would grease the slippery slope that would lead to the acceptance of abortion a few decades later.

Then, as now, it was the Catholic Church that stood firm not merely on the issue of contraception but also against the evils of communism and Nazism, even as many members of America's fashionable elites, Sanger and Little included, were fraternizing with one or the other of these murderous evils. On March 14, 1937, Pope Pius XI published his encyclical, *Mit Brennender Sorge* (With Burning Anxiety) against the evils of Nazism. With great courage, pastors read this from pulpits across Hitler's Reich on Palm Sunday (March 21), risking repercussions from Hitler's totalitarian regime. Almost simultaneously (on St. Joseph's Day, March 19), the pope issued another encyclical, *Divini Redemptoris*, condemning "atheistic communism," reiterating the Church's resistance to secularism in all its guises.

If the world at large had gone dark with devildom at the time of Tom Monaghan's entry into it, things were not much brighter closer to home. As his mother went into labor in Ann Arbor, the sixty-three thousand workers at the six Chrysler plants in nearby Detroit were in the midst of a major strike that would cost the company $26 million. On a lighter note, it was revealed on the day of Monaghan's birth that the Quaker Oats Company was paying the recently retired baseball giant Babe Ruth $25,000 per year to advertise its product. On the following day, the young Joe DiMaggio took the advice of Detroit Tigers legend Ty Cobb that he should replace his 40-ounce bat with a 36-ounce bat, and the rest, as they say, is baseball history.

New movies on March 25, 1937, included *Quality Street*, starring Katharine Hepburn; *The Amazing Adventure*, starring Cary Grant; and Frank Capra's *Lost Horizon*, starring Ronald Colman and Jane Wyatt. In the same year, Laurel and Hardy were *Way Out West*, and the Marx Brothers were spending *A Day at the Races*. The bestselling novel at the time was Margaret Mitchell's *Gone with the Wind*, published the previous year and soon to be made into a movie. Among the books published in 1937 were classics such as *The Citadel* by A. J. Cronin, *Of Mice and Men* by John Steinbeck, *The Hobbit* by J. R. R. Tolkien, and the first English-language edition of *The Diary of a Country Priest* by Georges Bernanos.

For a Catholic, however, the most significant thing about the date of Tom Monaghan's birth has nothing to do with the *year* in which he was born and everything to do with the *day*. March 25 is the most important day on the Christian calendar, more important than Christmas. It was on this day, the Feast of the Annunciation, that the Archangel Gabriel appeared to the Blessed Virgin Mary and announced that she was to bear a Child, the Son of God. This is the day, since life begins at conception and not at birth, that God became Man and that the Word became Flesh. This is the very date of the Incarnation.

As if this were not enough, March 25 was long considered the date of Christ's Crucifixion, a fact that we have forgotten due to Good Friday being celebrated as a moveable feast; this dating was universally accepted by the early Church because of those, such as the Blessed Virgin and St. John, who had witnessed the cataclysmic event and because of others, such as the cowardly disciples who had fled from the scene, who would always recall it, branded on their consciences, as their day of shame.

March 25 is, therefore, the date on which God became Man and also the date on which He died for our sins. Dates don't come any bigger and more charged with significance than that! It is for this reason that many countries in medieval Europe celebrated March 25 as New Year's Day. England and Wales celebrated it as such, calling March 25 "Lady Day," in honor of the Mother of God, until the Calendar Act of 1752 mandated January 1 as New Year's Day.

Since we are looking at the significance of the day on which Tom Monaghan was born, we should also note that March 25 is the feast day of St. Dismas, the Good Thief who was crucified with Christ. It can be said that all of humanity is on Golgotha with Christ—in one sense because it is our sins that nail Him to the Cross as well as in the sense that it is the weight of them which weighs Him down. There is, however, another sense in which all of humanity is on Golgotha with Christ, and that is in the sense that we all have our crosses to bear and in the sense that we are all crucified by the suffering that sin causes. Since we cannot avoid this cross and this suffering, it is only a question of how we respond to it. We can respond, like the bad thief, by blaming everybody but ourselves, including God, for the suffering in our lives, or we can respond, like the good thief, by accepting our suffering as the bitter fruit of our own sins and the sins of others and by asking God to forgive us and help us. The former condemns himself to a hell of his own making; the latter is promised a place in Paradise. There is, therefore, a sense in which St. Dismas serves as an everyman figure and, therefore, as a figure of Tom Monaghan also. Like St. Dismas, Monaghan is painfully aware of his sins and weaknesses and asks God for forgiveness and help.

There is also one other cause to ponder the significance of March 25, 1937, the day on which Tom Monaghan was born. In that particular year, March 25 fell on Holy Thursday, when the Church commemorates the Last Supper and when the Easter Triduum, the three most important days in the Church's year, begins. As such, Tom Monaghan's birthday is charged, as Gerard Manley Hopkins would say, with "the grandeur of God." None of this is to assert that Tom Monaghan has been "chosen" in any special way, beyond the sense in which it can be said that we are all "chosen"; nor is it to "anoint" him as a special one, beyond the sense in which we are all anointed at our baptism as special ones; nor is it (heaven forbid!) to canonize him, though he is called, like the rest of us, to be a saint. It is merely to suggest that we don't live in a world devoid of meaning and divorced from significance. It is not that our lives are written in the stars, as the astrologers believe, but that they are written in the Mind of the One who made the stars. There is a significance to our lives because there is a Signifier who guides us, should we wish to follow, with the hand of Providence.

Tom Monaghan would be remiss should he be blind to the manifold significance of the day on which he was born, and I would be remiss as his biographer were I to be blind to it. Well might he believe that the greatest birthday gift he has ever been given was the gift of the date on which he was born! The fact that the words of the Archangel on March 25—"Ave Maria"—have proved such an influence on Monaghan's life is no coincidence. He bears those theologically charged words as a birthmark and wears them, quite rightly, as a badge of honor. Well might he say, reversing the words of Mary, Queen of Scots, and T. S. Eliot, that in my beginning is my end.

CHAPTER 2

A TROUBLED CHILDHOOD

"HE'S WORTH a million dollars!" These were the words that Francis Monaghan is said to have exclaimed upon first setting eyes on his newborn son. Meant hyperbolically, they were not only prophetic but actually a significant understatement of what his son would one day be worth. At the time, however, the newborn was anything but a million-dollar baby, his parents having struggled to make ends meet in post-Depression Michigan and his father being already hampered by the health issues that would end his life a few short years later.

"My parents wanted me to be born on St. Patrick's Day, eight days earlier," says Tom, repeating stories he had heard from his relatives. "I'm sure they were disappointed when it didn't happen." The Irish roots ran deep. Tom's ancestors had arrived in the United States in the wake of the potato famine in the 1840s, his father's side apparently from Tipperary in the province of Munster, though the Monaghan family, or clan, seems to have its roots further north, in the province of Connacht. Tom is proud that "there was at least one nun in the family," a great-aunt on his father's side.

Stephen Monaghan, Tom's grandfather, married Mary Downs, whose ancestors are said to have come from Cork, even though most members of the Downs family who left Ireland following the famine had come to the United States from Sligo, to the north. "She was a big woman," Tom recalls, "very big. She's the reason my dad and his brothers were so big." Although she didn't finish high school, Mary Downs worked as a schoolteacher in a one-room schoolhouse for a while and was said to be a great storyteller, inheriting the gift of the blarney.

Stephen and Mary Monaghan had Francis (Tom's father), the first of their seven children, in 1912. After thirteen years of marriage, the couple separated and Mary left all seven children in the custody of her former husband. After Stephen Monaghan died (shortly after his wife had left him, the cause of death being evidently unknown), the raising of the family fell upon Francis, who, still only in eighth grade, was forced to abandon school and find himself a job so that he could support his younger brothers and sisters. He would grow into a fine young man, five feet eleven inches in height and 195 pounds. He was a good athlete, the ace pitcher for a traveling semiprofessional team. "Who knows," Tom wonders, "what he could have done in sports if he had the opportunity? My mother always talked about how big a man he was. I note that University of Michigan linemen at that time were no bigger than him." Tom also heard that his father had hoped to be a priest but that his desire had been thwarted by the abandonment of his schooling to support his brothers and sisters.

Toward the end of 1932, when Francis was twenty years old and working on a dairy farm, he met a seventeen-year-old girl, Anna Geddes, at a party. This was the beginning of a four-year courtship culminating in their marriage on April 14, 1936.

Anna's father, Warren Geddes, whose family was of Scottish descent, was brought up on a farm in Chelsea, Michigan, about fifteen miles west of Ann Arbor. He was a photographer who was part owner of four small movie theaters in the days of silent movies. He and his wife, Awema, whom he'd met when she was working as a waitress in a local restaurant, had two daughters, of whom Anna, born in 1915, was the elder. By the time that Frank and Anna met, Warren Geddes had been forced to sell his business, which fell victim to the Great Depression, and he never really had a job afterward. As such, Anna's family lived in poverty, in a small house that had no plumbing adjacent to the family farm. Her father did not own a car and walked into town every day to read the paper in the library and to check out a few magazines to bring home. Anna slept in the attic while her younger sister, Eva, slept in a large pantry closet behind the kitchen.

Although Francis Monaghan did not drink, due to the painful stomach ulcers that would ultimately cause his untimely death, his younger brothers drank heavily. Ed, the eldest of Francis's three brothers, was a small mason contractor, while Mike and Jack were bricklayers. Mike was around five feet ten and 170 pounds, whereas Jack, the youngest, was six feet four, big boned, and reputed to be the tallest man in Ann Arbor at that time. Jack and Mike were said to be the best bricklayers in town, regularly being placed first and second in the annual Labor Day bricklaying contest. Drink was their downfall. "Both died in their thirties of alcoholism," says Tom, "the Irish curse!"

Born a little over eleven months after his parents married, Tom's earliest memory, when he was about two years old, is of running after his father. "I wanted to be with him wherever he went," he recalls. Speaking with evident nostalgia, melding childhood memories with stories about his father that he heard later from family members, Tom's love for the parent who was snatched from him when he was so young remains undiminished: "There are so many memories that I have about my dad. Of course he's my hero. My aunts and uncles have talked about him in glowing terms. They probably embellished it, but I took it for fact. He'd give you the shirt off his back. He was a big man; he was an athletic guy."

Another memory is of the day that his father took him to see Michigan Stadium for the first time. Although it was not as large in 1940 as it is now (having a capacity of 85,752 compared with today's capacity of 109,901, making it the largest stadium in the United States and the second largest in the world), one can only imagine how huge it must have seemed to a three-year-old boy, holding the hand of his father, wide-eyed with wonder.

At the time, Francis Monaghan was working as a truck driver, driving a semitruck, and he'd often take his young son to the depot where he worked. Snippets of memory that Tom retains three-quarters of a century later include his helping his father put a little fire extinguisher in the door of the truck and also being given a bag of Spanish peanuts that his father had filled from a dispenser on the wall of the depot.

The three- or four-year-old drove everywhere with his father in the family's '37 Pontiac, but there was one particular occasion when his mother wouldn't let him go, though Tom has no recollection of the reason for his mother's refusal. As his father prepared to drive off, Tom crept to the back of the car, where an ice box was attached to the bumper (in those days it was common to buy a block of ice every day), and he climbed on, wedging himself between ice box and bumper. After several hundred yards of being bumped around as his father drove down the deeply rutted gravel road, the car finally pulled into a neighbor's driveway. Tom leapt down from his hiding place and ran to his father, shouting "Daddy! Daddy!," believing his father would be delighted to see him. Instead, his father was furious, no doubt frightened that his son could have been seriously hurt, and spanked him thoroughly, the only time that he ever punished him physically. Not wishing to get the boy into further trouble with his mother, his father kept this escapade a secret, saving Tom from a possible second spanking on the same day.

Tom recalls climbing on his father's back and how huge it seemed to be and, today, as an old man, he is still filled with nostalgia whenever he drives past the rocks on which he and his father used to climb on the bank of the river while swimming. On another occasion, his father was using a shovel down by the little creek alongside the house, possibly trying to divert the direction of the stream, not

noticing how close his son was behind him. As he swiv-
eled round, he thrust the shovel into the boy's stomach. "I
remember how concerned he was, though it really didn't
hurt me."

A special memory is of a time when he, his parents, and
his new baby brother, Jim, born in August 1939, were visiting relatives, his cousins on his mother's side, at their farm.
"They had a big drive, a round driveway with a windmill in
the middle, and there were two boys there, probably aged
around eighteen or nineteen, and somehow or other, they
must have challenged my dad to a race. So he raced them
across this area of about maybe a hundred feet or so, and
he won."

Tom slept in the same bed as his parents in the tiny
three-room house his father had built, and he remembers
his father getting up in the night to use the chamber pot
because the house did not have indoor plumbing. The
family used the water from the artesian spring for washing
and hauled drinking water from a neighbor's well. Eventually they had a well dug, and Tom's mother thought that
she was living the life of luxury when a hand pump was
installed in the kitchen sink. She prepared meals on a two-
burner electric hot plate and had only three cooking pans.
The three rooms were furnished with furniture donated by
Tom's aunts, and the solitary bed that the parents shared
with their two boys was a gift from his grandmother.

Fragments of conversation call to him across the
decades, including a discussion that his father was having
with his mother about motorcycles. His father said that
a three-wheeler motorcycle flipped over more easily than

a two-wheeler. "I remember being puzzled by that," says Tom, his young mind unable to grasp the counterintuitive nature of the strange fact presented to him.

Other splintered visions of memory include his father's pack of Lucky Strike cigarettes in his pocket—"that was back when it was green with a red circle"—and his father up a ladder banging nails into the siding of the house. "Dad never did finish that house," Tom would write many years later, "though he kept working on it whenever he could. I remember him talking enthusiastically about how someday he would build an addition for a bathroom and an extra bedroom."

The house itself was on a slight slope, and Tom recalls climbing into his father's car and somehow unwittingly knocking it out of gear or releasing the parking brake, causing the car to roll down the slope. "I was hanging on for dear life as the car rolled toward a four- or five-foot drop-off at a retaining wall, beyond which was a long slope running down to the Huron River. Luckily, the front wheels dropped into a shallow ditch that stopped the car just before the drop-off." Confessing the "crime" to his father and expecting to be punished, he was surprised when his father simply backed the car back up the slope. "He didn't say anything. He didn't chew me out or anything." This is typical of Tom's enshrined recollections of his father, whom he recalled as "a gentle man" who was always "very patient." "I don't think I could get enough of him . . . And when he'd come home, because he was on the road . . . I think he probably stayed away overnight a lot, and he was as far away as Cincinnati, which was a long ways in those days."

Tom's life with the gentle, patient man who was his hero came to a sudden, heartbreaking end on Christmas Eve 1941, when his father died of peritonitis, an infection of the lining of the abdomen caused by the perforated ulcers from which he had suffered for years. He was twenty-nine years old. His son was four. "I vaguely remember he was in the hospital and then being told that he had died. It was Christmas Eve—I remember a metal airplane, probably a DC-3 Model, under the tree with about an 18-inch wing-span." A few days later, he was taken to the funeral home. "I saw him lying there in the casket. I remember—all I remember is I saw him there, and I hadn't seen him for, what, three, four, five days. I missed him. And I went up to him, and I said, 'Daddy, wake up; wake up, wake up,' and I was screaming, and they pulled me out of there. When I saw him lying there, I guess I thought he was sleeping. 'Wake up, Daddy; wake up.'"

It took many months for the bereft and broken son to assimilate the death of his father, seeking solace in denial. "I remember when I was living in the foster home, a year after my father's death I guess, just sitting in the back of the car, going somewhere, you know, just thinking that, 'My daddy's coming back; he just—he just wouldn't leave me. He wouldn't do that to me.'"

One can only imagine how distraught Anna, Tom's mother, must have been at the sudden death of her husband, but her decision to place both of her sons into foster care remains a mystery. Why would she do such a thing, the effect of which was to deprive her sons of a mother's love so soon after losing the love of their father? The reason given to justify such an odd decision was that she couldn't afford to keep them on her weekly salary of $27.50, because her weekly expenses were $30. She needed to go back to school to become a registered nurse so that she could get a better-paying job, after which she would take her sons back to live with her again. Although this might seem reasonable enough, it doesn't really add up. She had received $2,000 in insurance after her husband's death, of which half was used to pay off the debt on the house. The other half was put into the bank as an "emergency fund." With $1,000 in the bank, a considerable sum in 1942, why couldn't she afford to keep her two sons with her? Even if her expenses continued to exceed her income by $2.50 per week, the money in the bank would still last almost eight years. The truth is that Anna's desertion of her two sons had little to do with her inability to manage financially and much more to do with her inability to cope psychologically. This much is suggested by Tom's own assessment of the situation. "She'd always had a difficult time managing me. She says that even when I was a baby, before I could walk—which I did at seven months—she couldn't leave me alone for a minute because I was so strong and restless that I'd pull the safety pins right out of my diapers. So she decided to put us into a foster home."

So it was that Tom, still not five years old, and Jim, still only two, were placed with foster parents. At first, they were passed from house to house, staying in each new home for only a week or two at a time. Eventually they were placed with a German couple, Frank and Maria Woppman, with whom the boys would stay for almost two years. "The Woppmans were very strict," Tom remembers. "The house was spotless. We had to take our shoes off in the house." Frank Woppman, whom Tom and his brother called Uncle Frank, was a sausage maker in a small grocery store. He and Maria spoke to each other in German and were always arguing. One can imagine the atmosphere being somewhat intimidating for the two young boys. On the brighter side, Maria Woppman was a good cook, preparing all their meals from scratch, and her husband spent much time in the garden, where he grew grapes from which he made wine. A vivid memory that stayed with Tom across the years was the outdoor parties at German Park, with the beer flowing as couples danced to a live band playing German *biergarten* music.

A major difference in life with the Woppmans, compared to the life the boys had lived with their parents, was that the Woppmans did not go to church on Sundays. Frank and Anna Monaghan had attended St. Thomas Catholic Church in Ann Arbor, and Tom remembers kneeling beside his father during Mass, but the Woppmans practiced no faith whatsoever. This struck Tom as being strange, and he asked Uncle Frank why they didn't go to church on Sunday. He was told that only bad people went to church, an explanation that Tom found unconvincing. "I was only five or six, but I didn't buy it."

During this period, Tom attended kindergarten at a public school and then began first grade. Halfway through the first grade, his mother decided to place him and Jim in St. Joseph's Home for Boys in Jackson, Michigan, about thirty-five miles due west of Ann Arbor, a Catholic orphanage run by the Felician sisters—all Polish from the old country. According to Tom, one of the reasons that his mother decided to move them to the orphanage was to have her sons raised in the Catholic faith. Anna Geddes had become a Catholic in order to marry Frank, and it's tempting to conjecture whether the decision to place her sons in the care of the Felicians was a mark of her own adherence to her adoptive faith or whether it was something she did to honor the memory of her deceased husband and to assuage her own conscience; alternatively, and more prosaically, one wonders whether she had other purely utilitarian or financial reasons for making the decision.

Whatever the reasons, Tom and Jim stayed at the orphanage for six years—until Tom was twelve years old. They were not very happy years, as Tom recalls: "Jackson was the home of the largest state prison in the US—nicknamed Jacktown. I've always said Jackson had two prisons, the other being St. Joe's Home. It was very strict. Everything was by the numbers. We all had a number. My number the last few years was 'twenty-five.' "

Upon arrival at the orphanage, on the very first day, Tom recalled "feeling intensely unhappy about my strange new surroundings." Uncharacteristically, he struck out at another boy for no apparent reason, no doubt needing to unleash his pent-up anger. "I confronted one boy who seemed repulsive to me. I'm not sure why, but he had some sort of cap or bandage on his head, and I found that so offensive that I hit him." Having vented his spleen against this unfortunate innocent victim, who would later become one of his friends, life settled down to a dull and dismal routine, which included the scrubbing and polishing of floors and the ironing of shirts and trousers "by the hundreds," all of which caused Tom to remember his time at the orphanage as "stifling."

For the remainder of first grade and all of second grade, Tom was taught in the orphanage itself. From the third grade onward, he was sent every day to St. Mary's, a local parish school. Now finding himself out in the wider world with "normal kids" who had "normal families," he began to feel self-conscious. "That's when I first started realizing how different I was. You know, everyone had a family. Everybody had nicer clothes, it seemed like."

It was, however, not all gloom and despondency, because he began to form a close relationship with one of the sisters, Sister Berarda, who would serve as a sort of surrogate mother in the absence of his real mother. He was under Sister Berarda's supervision upon his arrival at the orphanage and remained so throughout the first and second grades, at which time she was also his teacher. Under her guidance, supervision, and, above all, love, Tom thrived. There was "never any holding or hugging or anything," Tom recalls. "But I remember a warmth and encouragement and a smiling face. She didn't seem to think I could do anything wrong." He was the best student in the class and doing better than many of the students in the grades ahead of him. Sister Berarda was so impressed with his progress that she thought he might be able to skip the third grade, but his mother refused to give the necessary permission.

Unfortunately, from third grade onward, Tom no longer had the solace of Sister Berarda's care and attention, because he fell under the supervision of a new house mother, Sister Liadislaus, who ruled by the strap. "We were whipped for the slightest infraction; there was no leniency, never a reprieve. . . . We would have to pull down our pants, and she'd swing the strap with every ounce of strength she had." Tom described her as being "as tough as the strictest drill instructor I ever had in the Marine Corps." Under this new draconian regime, he lost interest in all aspects of life at the school, descending into what he described as "a gradual slump." "My school grades slid, and other kids started surpassing me in sports. . . . I managed to keep about a B average, as I recall, but I never regained the enthusiasm for classwork that Sister Beralda had given me."

One of the high points of these otherwise gloomy years was when the Knights of Columbus took the boys from the orphanage on the annual trip to Detroit to see the Tigers. These trips instilled in Tom a lifelong passion for the Tigers, which would not diminish with the passing of the years. "I have always been a big Tigers fan," he says. "It started with the winning of the world series in 1945 when I was eight years old. In the orphanage, we were all Tigers fans. I didn't even hear of the Detroit Lions until I was eleven or twelve." As none of the boys skated, there was little interest in the Red Wings. "It was all Tigers as far as professional sports teams go." The shared passion for baseball, and particularly for the Tigers, served as a bond that brought the boys of the orphanage together. "Our heroes were Hal Newhouser, Hank Greenberg, George Kell, Fred Hutchinson, Dizzy Trout, Virgil Trucks, and Hoot Evers. We knew the stats of all the players."

There was no TV at the orphanage, so Tom and the other boys would tune in regularly to WIBM to listen to the play-by-play commentary of the Tigers games by hall-of-fame legend Harry Heilmann. "We'd be glued to the radio during games. We couldn't wait for baseball season to start. We all had our favorite players. Mine was Hoot Evers." He imagined in his dreams playing shortstop for the Tigers when he grew up. Little could he have imagined, even in his wildest dreams, that he, a poor boy from the orphanage, would one day actually *own* the Tigers. It is one of the wonderful things about truth that it is all too often stranger than fiction and one of the great things about life that it is sometimes greater than our dreams.

In 1949, after six seemingly interminable years in the orphanage, the long-awaited release date arrived. Anna Monaghan had finally been able to buy a small house in Traverse City and wrote to tell her sons that they would soon be able to move in with her. The future finally began to look brighter for the optimistic and irrepressible twelve-year-old. "We were free. I was counting the days. I'd be able to get a job, save some money; the options were endless compared to my present situation." Things were looking up, or so it seemed. In fact, as Tom would soon discover, life with his mother would not be what he or she had hoped it would be. Life was not about to become a bowl of cherries, ripe for the picking, nor would it be a bed of roses, except for the thorns. As the naïve young man was about to discover, life was about to throw him another curve ball.

CHAPTER 3

A TROUBLED YOUTH

YEARS LATER, looking back to the days when he and Jim had finally moved in with their mother, Tom seemed almost haunted by the unpleasant memories that it still evoked. "I looked forward to the day that I could live with my mother, but when that happened, it was almost hell. She would go into tantrums—she had highs and lows like you wouldn't believe. For no reason, she would chase me around the room with a broom, screaming at me, even though I hadn't done anything." By comparison with this nightmare scenario, even the orphanage seemed relatively appealing. "She did us a favor by putting us there because living with her . . ." His voice trailed off. "It was a way of providing for us, and she was by herself, and she was not a very stable woman, and she could not handle two boys."

One senses, when talking to Tom about his mother or reading what he has said about her in the past, that there is always a struggle, deep within him, to understand the woman whose love he had craved as a child and who had always fallen short in providing him with the love and care that he needed. "When I went to live with her after I got out, I was embarrassed by her, which was not to my credit. The way she dressed, her hair, even the way she walked because she was flat-footed. And she was very spontaneous and childlike, and she had her swings where she'd just lose her temper." Asked whether these mood swings put him and his brother on edge because they never knew what to expect from one moment to the next, he answered in the affirmative but then added that "I think she treated me differently than she did my brother." Why was this? "I might have been a little more rambunctious. I was energetic. Some people say that I look so much like my dad. My grandma used to call me Little Francis." But why did that make her treat him any differently? Tom responded, almost dismissively, that he didn't know and then, as though to change the subject, he showed me some old family photographs so that I could see the resemblance between him and his father.

I asked Tom whether his mother was a tactile person, whether she ever hugged or kissed him. His answer was once again curiously off topic: "She was an incurable romantic in the sense that she certainly traveled, she loved to travel. She always said that she wished she were a man so she could be in the Merchant Marines. Her father owned the theater, and so she worked there all the time as an usher. She saw all the movies, and she talked about the movies all the time."

I wondered whether her desire to be in the Merchant Marines indicated that she felt trapped. Was being a mother and being in Michigan stifling her? Did she want the freedom to just wander off anytime she wanted? Might this have been part of the problem? Tom replied that he did not think "she was as maternal as most women are" and added that she traveled a lot when he and Jim were in the orphanage. "She went on vacations to a lot of places."

By herself?

"Or with friends."

But not with Tom or Jim?

"A little bit, but not—not a lot . . . She liked to see the world; she liked to travel."

Although Tom's relationship with his mother was problematic, to say the least, there were happier moments, mostly to be found outside the tense environment of the home. "I can recall how exciting it was to be free, to be able to go into stores by myself and look at the merchandise, to be allowed to have money in my pocket, to be able to make money. The transition from the regimentation of the orphanage to complete freedom . . . was exhilarating." Tom's lifelong interest in cars, which he had developed while staring at the automobiles on his twice-daily walks between school and orphanage—perhaps seeing in them a symbol of the freedom he craved—was exhibited in his unsuccessful efforts to find a job in one of the car dealerships in Traverse City. He had more success in finding summer jobs, most of which he took to keep him away from home and the interminable arguments he was having with his mother. He picked cherries for a while and, exhibiting the first traces of the entrepreneurial talents that would later transform his life, he would go fishing off the docks on Lake Michigan and then sell his catch door-to-door after cleaning it. He also grew vegetables in a little garden patch at home, selling these door-to-door as well, and tried his hand at hawking the local newspaper on street corners.

On Sundays, the family attended Immaculate Conception Catholic Church in Traverse City, and Tom befriended the pastor, Fr. Russell Passeno, who would become a surrogate father to the disoriented boy. "During this period," Tom wrote, "religion became increasingly important to me." He missed the "clockwork of rituals" to which he'd become accustomed at the orphanage, seeking some structure to his somewhat dysfunctional life. "Not that I was devout—I wasn't. But I felt that religion was the one thread of continuity in my life." He never missed Mass on Sunday and served at the altar, having been well prepared at the orphanage where he had been taught to be an altar boy and learned the necessary Latin as early as the second grade.

Fr. Passeno—who was himself new to the parish, having taken over as pastor of Immaculate Conception in 1948, only a year before Tom's arrival—was a great help during this difficult period, offering encouragement and helping Tom smooth out the ongoing problems in his relationship with his mother. He also hired Tom to do odd jobs around the church and the school, paying him 35 cents per hour, which supplemented the 60 cents a day that Tom was earning selling newspapers. As a mark of his affection for the parish priest who, in his own estimation, "was the closest thing to a father figure I had," Tom bought him as a Christmas present a Fostoria frosted-crystal Madonna that he had spotted in the window of a local jewelry store. It cost $7.50, a considerable sum for a boy working odd jobs for relatively little money, but Tom evidently thought it a small price to pay to show his affection and appreciation for Fr. Passeno. "It seemed every penny I made that first year went to Christmas presents for Jim, Ma, and Fr. Passeno."

In spite of his best efforts, Tom's problems with his mother were not getting any better; if anything, they were getting worse. They fought constantly. Finally, unable to cope, she applied to the state Children's Home and Aid Society to have him placed in a foster home. Tom was sent to live on a farm with a family named Beaman in Interlochen, about fifteen miles southwest of Traverse City, where he stayed for the remainder of the school year and most of the following summer. When school resumed, he was sent, along with Jim, to live on another nearby farm with a family named Johnson. A few months later, Jim returned home to his mother while Tom was sent to another, smaller farm along the Boardman River owned by a Mr. and Mrs. Crouch. It had no electricity or indoor plumbing and no heating except for a wood stove in a downstairs room. It was, to the teenage boy, "a very humble but, to my way of thinking, wonderful place." He loved everything about life on a small working farm. He enjoyed getting up early in the morning to help with the chores and learned to milk cows, pitch hay, chop wood for kindling, and shovel manure.

Although he enjoyed life on the farm, he was already thinking of bigger, if not necessarily better things. By the light of a gas lantern in the Crouch farm he read a book about the childhood of Abraham Lincoln. "His story inspired me to dream big." If a poor farm boy from Illinois could work hard and become president of the United

States, why should he, a poor farm boy from Michigan, put limits on himself? He dreamed of being wealthy enough to build himself a house or cabin, his later love of architecture already showing itself, and would furnish it in his imagination with the items he found in mail order catalogues. His dreams were also furnished during the mile-and-a-quarter walk every morning to catch the school bus, during which he would imagine himself being rich and successful, perhaps as a great architect like Frank Lloyd Wright.

Another fascination for the adolescent boy was his obsession with girls. "My obsession with girls was kind of odd, considering the fact that I was so shy I could scarcely say hello to the ones I liked, not to mention that they seemed to have no interest at all in me. But of course, that didn't deter me from dreaming about them." One particularly pretty girl on whom he had "a big crush" was the girl who sat in front of him in class. Overcoming his shyness, he called her up to ask her for a date. She said, "Just a moment," and kept him waiting for what seemed an eternity. Finally, she came back to the phone and told him that her mother thought she was too young to go out on dates.

One of the reasons for his shyness, and one of the reasons that he believed that the girls at his school were not interested in him, was that he was poor. "I was embarrassed by my worn clothes; I usually had holes in my socks and the soles of my shoes. I was girl crazy, but I felt they were unattainable because of my circumstances."

The newfound discovery of girls had eclipsed the belief that he had a vocation to the priesthood, a belief that he had nursed and nurtured since second grade. Ever since first learning to serve at Mass in his earliest days at the orphanage, he had presumed that he would enter the seminary when he reached the ninth grade. Although the pretty girl who sat in front of him in school had "changed all that," as he would write later, the call to the priesthood, or at least the pull toward the priesthood, returned during the spring of his freshman year at high school. In what he would refer to as a "moment of revelation" while he was shoveling manure on the Crouch farm, he realized that he wasn't being true to himself. "The symbolism of the situation was overpowering: Standing up to my ankles in muck, I saw that I had been wallowing in crass, worldly thoughts when I should have been concentrating on my spiritual quest. I decided then and there that I would become a priest." He took his desire and sense of resolution to Fr. Passeno, who listened sympathetically to his story and agreed to help him apply to the seminary in Grand Rapids. The question on the application form asked the applicant why he wanted to become a priest. Tom answered that he sought the salvation of souls. "It's ironic," he would write more than sixty years later, "but that's the entire purpose of my work and life today. My own soul included, of course."

Although he was now in tenth grade and would therefore be a year behind the other boys, he felt confident that he could make it up and was elated when he was accepted. Fr. Passeno cautioned the fourteen-year-old that he might find the adjustment to the seminary difficult, "but neither he nor I had any inkling of what a disaster I would be as a seminarian."

At first, things went smoothly enough. Unlike most of the other boys, he was not homesick, and the six years in the orphanage had prepared him well, or so he thought, for the institutional life that the seminary entailed. Years later, his view had changed. "The problem, as I see it now, was the similarity between the discipline of the seminary and that which I had disliked so much in the orphanage. I had grown adept at sidestepping rules in the orphanage, and I didn't take the regulations of St. Joseph's [Seminary] seriously enough." Although he was doing well enough in his studies, struggling with Greek but attaining a perfect score on one of the religion tests, he tended to be mischievous, getting into pillow fights, acting rambunctious, and being reprimanded for talking in the study hall. He was occasionally late for class or chapel.

The final straw for the rector appeared to be a letter that he'd received from Tom's mother complaining that Tom wasn't writing to her often enough. In truth, Tom wrote more often to his aunt Peg in Ann Arbor "who was more of a mother to me." Holding the letter in his hand, the rector was furious at what he perceived, naturally enough, to be neglectfulness on Tom's part toward his parent. The rector, of course, only knew half the story—less than half—and couldn't have been expected to make a judgment based on Anna Monaghan's woeful neglect of her son, about which he presumably knew little or nothing. Shortly afterward, Tom was told to pack his bags. His life as a Catholic seminarian was at an end. "I lasted less than a year. Never before or since have I felt so crushed. I am no stranger to failure, but no other setback devastated me as this one did, because it was so final."

There is a sense that, decades later, Tom still harbored something of a grudge toward his mother for writing that letter. And yet, truth be told—as he readily admits—he was seldom out of trouble. It was expected that a student might be called to the rector's office on some disciplinary matter around four times a year. In his first year, Tom had been to the rector's office eleven times. In this sense, the cause for his dismissal cannot be blamed exclusively on the offending letter, even if it was the final straw.

In another sense, however, his mother can be blamed, at least in part. Most of the seminarians were from good homes and no doubt, and in consequence, were better behaved. The prefects who monitored the behavior of the new students were upperclassmen, also probably from good homes, who doubtless looked disdainfully at the unruly behavior of the kid from the wrong side of the tracks who couldn't seem to keep himself out of trouble. Tom described himself as "a little bit of a hell-raiser" during his time at the seminary, and one can only imagine how such behavior was received by some of the straight-laced students. Unlike these more fortunate young men, Tom's troubled childhood and his equally troubled youth were proving to be his downfall.

CHAPTER 4

TRUST AND ITS BETRAYAL

HAVING BEEN dismissed ignominiously from seminary, Tom dragged himself home to his mother like a dog with its tail between its legs. Resenting what he perceived as his mother's role in his dismissal, he was not inclined to make much of an effort with their troubled relationship. In order to avoid the constant bickering, he stayed away from home as much as possible, finding solace in the evenings setting pins at a local bowling alley.

His relationship with his mother plumbed new depths after he borrowed her car without permission and without telling her where he was going. Frantic with fear or anger, or both, she called the police. Failing to accept that he had done anything wrong and believing that his mother had betrayed his trust in calling the police, he obstinately refused to apologize even though his obstinacy resulted in a night in jail.

Things would get worse. One day, when Tom was on his way home from basketball practice after school, a car pulled up to the curb beside him. The driver rolled down the window and called to him, asking him if his name was

Monaghan. "Yeah," Tom replied. "What's up?" The man flashed a badge that said "county sheriff" and told Tom to get in the car. He was taken home to get his clothes and told that he was being taken to live in a detention home.

"I was in shock," Tom remembered. "It was like some awful nightmare." He hadn't committed any crime and couldn't believe that he was being put in a home for juvenile delinquents. He was told that his mother had signed the order to have him detained because she couldn't put up with him any longer. He spent the first night in the cell, his anger welling up inside him. "I couldn't believe it. I was furious. I didn't sleep a wink all night. I hollered and made a commotion all night long, screaming that I wasn't a crook."

The next day he was taken to the detention home, which was run by a policeman and his wife. There were about a dozen other youths there, many of whom had real problems. Up till then, Tom, who was seventeen, had no idea that "kids could be so bad." Stealing was endemic, and he learned to hide everything that he couldn't keep on his person. He had no intention of emulating their bad example, nor of plummeting into a downward spiral of petty crime or worse. "I was ashamed. I didn't know how I would face the other kids at school after they learned I was in the detention home with a bunch of juvenile delinquents and some real criminals." He decided that he would avoid the problem by not telling anyone and by walking to school via a circuitous route that took him close to his mother's house. His basketball coach helped, enabling him to go to practices and games. The ruse worked, because his class-mates never discovered his shameful secret.

When his aunt Peg and uncle Dan in Ann Arbor dis-covered the situation, they got custody of him from a judge, and after six months in the detention home, he moved in with them. "I was treated like a member of the family," says Tom, "and that's what I had craved ever since I first went to the orphanage." He loved it when aunt Peg told him stories of his father's boyhood, and he began to feel that, for the first time since his father's death, he was leading a normal life. He was not, however, excelling as a student at St. Thomas High School in Ann Arbor, and it looked doubtful for a time whether he would graduate. He had ceased taking an interest in his lessons ever since being sent home from the seminary, and something of the frustra-tion he felt, mingled with inarticulate hopes for the future, could be detected in the caption under his picture in the class yearbook: "The harder I try to be good, the worse I get; but I may do something sensational yet."

Graduating at the very bottom of his class, Tom moved into a rented room in Ann Arbor for six dollars a week and found employment with a newspaper and magazine distribution company. He got around with a used bike he purchased for thirty-eight dollars. Other dead-end jobs fol-lowed. He worked as a flagman on a highway asphalting job, he dug ditches for Ann Arbor's city water department, and he worked as an orderly at the University of Michigan hospital. He was going nowhere and decided to pursue his boyhood dream of becoming an architect. Having saved about five hundred dollars, he enrolled at Ferris Institute, now Ferris State University, but found it difficult to survive financially. Sharing the upstairs of a house off campus with seven other students, two to a room, he didn't even have enough money for food after paying for tuition and books; one week, he lived almost entirely on popcorn that had been around for a long time and a bottle of wine he found in the cupboard.

Tom did well enough in the exams at Ferris to be accepted at the University of Michigan the following year. It was a great leap forward academically but would be much more expensive. His only hope was to find a well-paid job in the summer and, finding nothing suitable in Ann Arbor or Detroit, he decided to hitchhike to Chicago. He was picked up by a man with a trucking company. After they had chatted for a while, the man offered his young passenger a well-paid job, which would include the free use of a car. Tom could not believe his luck. He had hit the jackpot. Or so he thought. Soon they were driving down country gravel roads, and the man pulled over to buy some beer. A little later, he stopped the car, put his hand on Tom's leg and propositioned him. Shocked at the strange turn of events, Tom grabbed his suitcase, walked a long way on small country roads to a main highway, found a motel, and spent the night. The next day, chastened by the weird experience of the night before and the naïve way in which he'd trusted the stranger, he hitchhiked the rest of the way to Chicago.

Arriving in the southern suburb of Harvey, Tom booked himself into a room in a rundown hotel for ten dollars a week, for which he paid by setting pins at a bowling alley at night while looking for the elusive well-paid job by day. As the summer slipped by, it became evident that he would not be able to save enough money to enroll at the University of Michigan in the fall. In desperation and what appears in hindsight to be a moment of reckless spontaneity, he enlisted with the Marine Corps. When he did so, he thought he was joining the army. He was told if he served for three years, he would get two years of college. During the week or so before he and his fellow recruits were shipped to San Diego for boot camp, Tom explored Chicago, the sheer size of the city beguiling the small-town boy from Michigan. He saw all the major sights and went to the movies, seeing Burt Lancaster, Gina Lollobrigida, and the young Tony Curtis in *Trapeze*. Having befriended another marine recruit, they went to a burlesque theater to see a strip show. Remembering this period of uncharacteristic ribaldry with the other recruit, Tom remarks that he doesn't know who was a bad influence on whom.

Boot camp in Southern California followed, and Tom was shocked and initially indignant at the habitual swearing of the drill instructors and other marines. "How could I respect these people who talked that way? It seemed that the *F* word was part of every sentence, used as a noun, adjective, and verb." Peer pressure being what it is, he was soon swearing like a sailor (or marine) himself. "The only thing I can say is I never used the name of God in vain. At least that much of my upbringing came out." As he developed bad habits, the most important of his good habits, regular Mass attendance, was lost. Nobody in his barracks went to Mass, and one Sunday, after a heavy night of drinking the night before, he decided to stay in bed instead of getting up and walking the mile or so across camp to Mass. Having broken the habit of a lifetime, he began to occasionally skip Mass on Sundays. This intermittent Mass attendance continued for about six months until he picked up a book by G. G. Greenwood entitled *The Faith of an Agnostic*. Considering that Greenwood's thesis was antithetical to Christian orthodoxy and openly hostile to Catholicism, it is ironic that the young marine was brought back to the practice of the Catholic faith by his reading of this book. Thereafter, having presumably seen through the inadequacies of Greenwood's agnosticism, Tom never had any further serious doubts about his Catholic faith and has practiced it ever since.

According to his own estimation, boot camp was "hell." Many didn't make it. One who did was a certain Lee Harvey Oswald, later to win notoriety for assassinating President John F. Kennedy. Tom remembers Oswald as "a little guy, very quiet and even a little strange." Oswald lined up next to Tom in formation and was in the same eight-man tent with him during boot camp. Although he spent quite a lot of time with him, Tom can't relate too much about him because he was "pretty quiet" and kept to himself, already showing signs of being the loner who would defect to the Soviet Union three years later.

Following boot camp and advanced infantry training, Tom was shipped to Okinawa, then to mainland Japan, and then back to Okinawa before returning to the United States, spending the last year of service at Camp Pendleton in Southern California.

During this period, in his bunk aboard ship in the mid-Pacific, the young marine found himself pondering the meaning of life. He had always been a daydreamer, imagining the day when he would be successful in whatever future life his flights of fancy dreamed up for him. Now, daydreaming in the middle of the ocean, thousands of miles from wherever his home might be, he realized that all this fantasizing was ultimately meaningless. Yet if his daydreams lacked meaning, what, if anything, did have meaning? This set him thinking. If money, fame, and creature comforts could not bring happiness and fulfillment, where was such happiness to be found? "I realized that if I lost my health, I'd gladly give all the money I had to get my health back. So retaining my health had to be a higher priority." And yet physical health in the absence of a strong intellectual understanding of things would also be meaningless. Thus intellectual or mental health, the life of the mind, was also important. Yet even that in itself could not bring happiness and meaning to one's life. What one needs are relationships. One needs to be a good husband, a good father. One needs to love and be loved. "Now I'm getting somewhere!" he thought. It was as though a light was being switched on and that he was being shown a road map of how to live a good and meaningful life: "A set of priorities by which to conduct my life: social, mental, physical, and *then* financial. Wow! But there's one more thing. Someday, I'm going to die. As I've been taught through my Catholic faith, I'm going to spend eternity in heaven or hell, depending on how I lived my life. As the nuns said many times, echoing the words of Christ, 'What does it profit a

man if he gains the whole world but loses his soul?' I had
left out the most important priority: the spiritual."

And so the young marine, lying in his bunk and staring pensively at the ceiling, had stumbled upon, or perhaps
had been providentially guided to, the five priorities that
would govern his life: spiritual, social, mental, physical,
and financial. Although the financial area of life came last
in the order of priorities, it still had an important place.
"Always being ambitious, I wanted to include the financial
goal," Tom explains. "I found a way to do it. Put it in its
place. Money is not in itself evil. It's neutral. The *love* of
money is evil. Money buys many good things: hospitals,
Bibles, churches, et cetera. It's a tool to do good in the right
person's hands. By having one's priorities straight, money
can serve a good purpose."

Having ascertained the five priorities, he could now
use them as a practical guide to leading a good life. The
first priority, the *spiritual*, meant that he had to be a good
Catholic; the second priority, the *social*, meant that, if he
got married, he needed to be a good husband and father
and that, until then, he needed to be a good person, loving his neighbor and being open to everyone he met; the
mental priority meant that he had to be in the habit of
reading the right sort of books to enable him to lead a good
life by accomplishing the five priorities; the *physical* priority meant that he needed to always take care of his health,
through exercise, a good diet, and the control of his weight.
Last in the pecking order of these life priorities was the
financial aspect, which was nonetheless still important and

would mean that he must always work hard and find ways of saving his earnings.

The formulation of these priorities, and the practical resolutions that they demanded, was quite literally life changing. "I hate to think where my life would be if I didn't have this road map," Tom says, looking back across the half century and more that has passed since then. In retrospect, he feels that he has worked on all five areas and has clearly been successful in the last two, being in astonishingly good physical health and having made billions of dollars throughout his life. He is also "trying to make progress in the first three areas, especially the spiritual," adding whimsically that "on that one, I've got a ways to go. I hope I have time!"

While in the Marines, and showing a much greater degree of prudence than most men of his age, Tom saved about half of his income, having it withdrawn automatically from his pay and sent to a mutual fund in Ann Arbor. As his discharge date approached, he had all sorts of exciting plans on how he would use the two thousand dollars he had saved. This was a considerable sum of money in 1959, and the twenty-two-year-old intended to use it to build a new and better life for himself. Unfortunately, however, the prudence he exhibited in saving the money was lacking in the manner in which he chose to invest it. Hitchhiking back to base, he was picked up by a man in a brand-new Buick who claimed to be a bigshot in the oil industry. By the time they had reached the base, this man, who introduced himself as John Patrick Ryan, had persuaded Tom to invest five hundred dollars with him. Within a month or two, Ryan had convinced the young marine that he was on the verge of a big deal and needed more capital to seal it, making his new "business partner" an offer that was too good to be true. "I fell for it," Tom confesses, "and wound up loaning him the remainder of my savings, plus my three hundred dollars or so of mustering-out pay." Having been betrayed once again by those in whom he'd invested his trust, Tom was forced to hitchhike the two thousand and more miles from Southern California to Michigan with nothing but fifteen dollars in his pocket and to his name.

At this juncture, it would be good to look at the trust-fulness that Tom showed to the disreputable liar who had picked him up when he was hitchhiking and the trust that he would later show to those equally disreputable people whom he would trust as business partners after he started Domino's. In his biography, James Leonard seems to gloat at the fact that Tom was hoodwinked repeatedly by con men who, as business partners, took him for a ride and, occasionally, to the cleaners. According to Leonard, "the worst mistake a businessman can make [is] trusting untrust-worthy people" (349). Three early chapters in Leonard's book are titled, in sequence, "Fool Me Once," "Fool Me Twice," and "Fool Me Three Times," alluding to the idiom, "fool me once, shame on you; fool me twice, shame on me." The point that Leonard is making is that anyone can be taken in once but that only a fool is taken in twice and, by extension, only a complete idiot could be taken in three times. Tom Monaghan is, therefore, in Leonard's estima-tion, a complete idiot for being so gullible in his dealings with people, and we are meant to join him in pointing the finger of scorn at the idiot.

The question that is begged, of course, is how could someone so dumb become so successful? Part of the reason has to be an openness to opportunity, which is rooted in an optimism about the world and the people in it. Cynics who trust nobody are trusted by nobody, nor do they make many friends. The delinquent teenagers with whom Tom lived in the detention home were cynical enough to be "streetwise" and would no doubt be "smart" enough to not be fooled even once, let alone twice. In consequence, they would not form lasting friendships, or any other position of trust for any length of time, dooming themselves to become life's loveless "losers." Tom escaped their fate because he refused to abandon the sense of morality that he'd learned from Sister Berarda, Fr. Passeno, and others, and continued to see the goodness in people, all of whom he believed were made in the image of God, though broken by sin. There is no room in such a creed for the coldblooded and coldhearted cynicism that treats human beings as fools to be preyed upon. The price for such openness, which theologians would call charity, is sometimes a susceptibility to trust those whom we should not trust. Considering the alternative, it is a small price to pay.

Recognizing the problem, Tom acknowledges that "part of the fault" in these situations is his. "I am slow to recognize dishonesty in others because I prefer to trust people. I look for the good in others, not the bad." Larry Sperling, Tom's first attorney in the early days of Domino's, summed up the paradox in an interview with James Leonard by stating that Tom was "a simple, straightforward guy" and "a highly moral individual, not a dirty player," which meant that "it often took him a while to figure somebody out." He was sometimes "impressed by flash and easily taken in." And yet, in spite of the dangers that such credulity could and did present, the trust that he had in others engendered trust in others toward him, helping him build enduring and fruitful friendships. "Nobody can succeed in business without the help of friends," Tom stresses. "And that probably goes double in franchising, where trust is the grease that keeps the working parts from binding."

It is true that Tom learned the hard way that there are people in the world who do nasty things but equally true that he got better at spotting them before too much damage was done to him or his business. It is also true that he built a hugely successful global corporation in spite of such naivety or gullibility and, one might be tempted to say, that he built it, at least in part, *because* of such trust in people and the openness to seeing the good in them. He had been embattled the whole of his young life, and occasionally battered, but never did he become embittered. Had he done so—had he closed his heart to the love of neighbor, refusing to trust anyone in case he should be "fooled twice"—he would have become the sort of small-minded and hard-hearted person who achieves little and whose human relationships fail and falter. Well might Tom Monaghan be thankful that he retained trust in his fellow man in spite of the frequent betrayal of that trust from his earliest years.

CHAPTER 5

FROM SKID ROW
TO MAKING DOUGH

TOM WAS never more down and out than during the long hitchhike home from California to Michigan in the summer of 1959. Having lost his hard earned savings to a con man, he found himself in Denver, penniless and without a place to sleep. He went to Travelers Aid, and there the staff sent him to a mission. "It was on skid row, in the vicinity of Larimer Street, and was full of derelicts, mostly old men who seemed to be alcoholics." Taking one look at the place, Tom decided to leave. To his horror, he was informed that it was too late because the door had been locked for the night. He had no choice but to stay until morning. He had lived in an orphanage and a detention home and had spent a couple of nights in police cells, but nothing was as bad as this. He and the other homeless "inmates" were made to take a shower in filthy stalls and were then handed hospital-type nightgowns. It was then, Tom remembers, that things "got really creepy." Many of the elderly men were apparently homosexuals who began to proposition the young man in their midst with lewd comments. Unable to escape the nightmare scenario, he lay awake all night on the dirty sheets, tensed up and ready to lash out at anyone who touched him. No one did so, but the fear was enough to prevent him sleeping a wink. He bolted as soon as the door was unbolted at 6 a.m., not hanging around for breakfast in spite of his hunger and his inability to buy himself food. The hellish night represented a new low point in the young man's life, branding him with an enduring sympathy for the homeless and anyone who has no choice but to endure such places. "I'll never forget that experience," he says, "and I feel sorry for people who are so down and out that they have to go to a place like that."

Having found a couple of weeks' work in the Denver area to put some money in his pockets, he finally managed to make his way back to Michigan. By this time his mother had remarried and had moved back to Ann Arbor, and his brother, Jim, who was working for the post office, was renting two attic rooms in a house in town. Jim allowed Tom to stay with him while he found his feet and gave him an old rusted-out '49 Plymouth, which Tom appreciated. For a time, Jim worked in the evenings at McDonald's in Ann Arbor, one of the early stores of the burgeoning fast-food giant, which was spreading its empire across the United States from its original home base in California. Tom was intrigued by the place and the way it did business and made lots of money. "I used to go in there a lot," he says. "I was intrigued with the operation, how much money they were making, how streamlined they were, the hamburgers, french fries, shakes. Everything about it. I was especially intrigued by the simplicity of it."

If his experience of the new vogue for fast food had fired Tom's imagination, sowing seeds for the future, he was still determined at this point to further his education. Once again, he had been accepted by the University of Michigan, and once again, his ability to attend was being compromised by a lack of funds. He found work as a home-delivery manager for a local news agency and hoped that the income would be sufficient to see him through the first semester. He started classes with a sense of apprehension that he might not be able to hold down his job and do the required coursework. To make matters worse, he couldn't afford to buy the required textbooks and hoped that paying close attention in class, coupled with a diligent use of the library and occasionally borrowing books from other students, would be enough to get him by. It wasn't. He began to fall behind. As if this were not enough with which to cope, he was suffering from an excruciating earache, which turned out to be caused by a ruptured and infected eardrum. Having little option, he pulled out of classes, planning to enroll in the following semester, by which time he presumed that his eardrum and his personal finances would both be healthier. In the event, his return to the University of Michigan in the spring semester was no more successful. Again, he lasted only three weeks. This time he was forced to withdraw because of the size of the payments on the '55 Ford station wagon he had bought in order to deliver papers and also because some of the courses, notably calculus, were way over his head.

In September 1960, Tom's brother approached him with a proposal for a business partnership that was destined to change his life in the most dramatic fashion. Jim had discovered that DomiNick's, a pizza store in Ypsilanti, just to the east of Ann Arbor, was up for sale. The asking price was five hundred dollars down. Neither Jim nor Tom had that sort of money, but Jim paid seventy-five dollars as a down payment, and the remainder was loaned from the post office credit union. The store was theirs. Tom and Jim Monaghan were in business, and in debt, as pizza entrepreneurs, assuming a large note.

The brothers opened doors on the new store, which was still called DomiNick's (Monaghan's Pizza not having the necessary Italian ring) on December 9, 1960. It was a day later than planned because the previous day was the feast of the Immaculate Conception, a holy day of obligation, which meant that Tom needed to go to Mass on the evening of the eighth. The practice of the faith was once again an integral part of his life, the first in his list of priorities, and, this being so, he struggled with the idea of opening the store on Sundays. This was a real dilemma. The dorms at nearby Eastern Michigan University didn't serve meals on Sunday, making it the busiest day of the week for the pizza store. Tom took the problem to a local priest who reassured him that there was no moral problem with DomiNick's opening on Sundays under such circumstances.

The first practical problem was that Tom had no idea how to make a pizza. Dominick DeVarti, the previous owner of the store, gave him a quick fifteen-minute lesson—a sort of pizza-making for dummies—and then he was on his own. Practice makes perfect, however, and within a few weeks he was tossing the pizza dough like an old hand.

The Monaghan-owned DomiNick's made an inauspicious start. Jim got cold feet and wouldn't give up the security of his job at the post office, leaving Tom to effectively run the business by himself. In the first week, the store grossed only ninety-nine dollars. In hindsight, Tom feels that it was amazing that the business survived. "I was working almost every waking hour of the day and losing money every week." The bills were piling up, and he was once again living penuriously. He rented a room across the street from the store and lived on scraps of food. For the first half of 1961, most of his meals were burnt or leftover pizzas that had never been picked up by customers, supplemented by leftover, unsold pies from the bakery next store. Occasionally, he would get a free meal from a friend's mother who would have him over once in a while, though never from his own mother who was now living locally with her new husband. He could no longer afford to run a car, selling the '55 Ford station wagon.

By the middle of the year, Jim had seen enough. He wanted to dissolve the partnership, not seeking anything for his half of the business, which was, in any case, worth nothing. In an act of great generosity, considering his own poverty-stricken predicament, Tom felt that his brother deserved something for taking the initial risk in starting the business and offered to give him the two-year-old Volkswagen that they had recently purchased to make deliveries. "So I gave it to him, and I kept making the payments. That's how I bought 50 percent of what became Domino's Pizza."

Business picked up in September 1961, when the students returned for the fall semester, but not enough to make a profit. The store was busy every night, and there were rushes that the small and inexperienced staff could not handle, getting very behind with orders. Tom described life at this time as a "rat race." He would spend all day preparing for the evening, making dough and grinding cheese, and then not being able to handle the rush when it came. "It seemed we could never quite get our act together."

Slowly things began to pick up, partly because Tom was getting better at making pizzas and at being a pizza entrepreneur, and partly because of the simplification of the menu, offering fewer options, a strategy that would serve Domino's Pizza well in the years ahead. By the end of 1961, a year after the doors of the Monaghan-owned DomiNick's Pizza had opened, sales were reaching $1,500 a week, with a weekly profit of $400. If this surge in sales could be maintained, the business would be making more than $20,000 a year, a reasonably decent income.

Things were looking up but they were not looking up high enough for the ambitious entrepreneur for whom the sky was the limit, or perhaps even the stars. Why settle for only one store? Why not aim to start a whole chain of stores in other college towns? With this idea in mind, and with the stars in his eyes, he planned to open a second store in Mount Pleasant, near the campus of Central Michigan University. To help him with this expansion plan, he went into partnership with Jim Gilmore, an older man whom he felt he could trust. Gilmore, whom Tom described as "a witty little Irishman who had a twinkle in his eye and a gift for one-liners that kept customers chuckling," was fifty-one years old, twice Tom's age, and experienced in the pizza business. He had founded Pizza from the Prop, Ann Arbor's best-known pizzeria, which had gone bankrupt, largely because Gilmore was an alcoholic. At the time that he and Tom had met, Gilmore had joined Alcoholics Anonymous and was on the wagon. Against his better judgment, and perhaps as blinded by the blarney as he had been in his earlier encounter with the man who called himself John Patrick Ryan, Tom agreed to give Gilmore a 50 percent stake in the business for only five hundred dollars, in spite of the fact that Tom now believed the business to be worth about twenty thousand dollars. He justified the generous nature of the deal with Gilmore on the basis that he needed someone with experience to help him with the plans to purchase the new store in Mount Pleasant and possibly other stores thereafter. "I figured that with his brains and experience (he had been in the restaurant business his entire life, before getting into the pizza business) and my hard work, it'd be a good partnership." If the business continued to grow, Tom reasoned, it would not matter what percentage of the company he owned, nor what amount Gilmore had paid him for his half of it. As reasonable as this might have seemed, the decision to go into partnership with Gilmore proved a costly mistake. In Monaghan's words, it "turned out to be the most lopsided partnership in the history of American business, largely because no one would put up with what I did over the next three years. To start with, he *never* paid me the five hundred dollars."

If Gilmore wasn't exactly a con man like John Patrick Ryan, he was certainly a freeloader who made a loss with every aspect of the business that he managed while still paying himself generously out of the profits that Tom's half of the business was making. It was essentially a parasitic relationship, Tom making the money and living frugally while Gilmore spent the money that Tom had made, living a life of luxury. After three years of this "lopsided partnership," Tom finally did something about it. "I was angry. It was like three years of holding it in, and then I could not stand it any longer. He lived like a king while I was living in a trailer." Gilmore had been taking advantage of him this whole time, and Tom finally demanded the ending of their partnership. Although the legal aspects of their unorthodox partnership were complicated, the two men eventually agreed that Gilmore could have the two pizza restaurants in Ann Arbor while Tom would have the three pizza stores that he had by this time opened. Whereas Tom's pizza business continued to prosper, Gilmore's restaurants floundered, and he was declared bankrupt within a year or so. He died about five years later, probably from health issues connected to his years of alcohol abuse. "I felt sorry for him," Tom says, "despite all the trouble he caused me. He was an unforgettable character, and in his own strange way, he did make a contribution to the growth of Domino's."

One effect of Tom's budding success as an entrepreneur was the suspension of all facets of his social life. After his return to Ann Arbor following his time in the Marines, he was in the habit of going to the Newman Club on the University of Michigan campus, where he got to know the Catholic students. He dated several girls whom he met there, taking them to Red's Right Spot, a favorite student hangout (which was also where he first met Jim Gilmore, who had been working there as a chef). He had not dated many girls up to this point in his life and his motives when doing so were not always pure or good. By his own admission he was "no saint" where his relationship with girls was concerned and, as he put it to me, he wouldn't want his eternity to be based on what he did in his relationships with girls before he met Margie, the woman who would become his wife and the mother of his four daughters. "I was not as wild as I wanted to be," he remarks on his experiences with the opposite sex prior to his marriage. "The reason I wasn't wilder than I was is because I was terribly shy of girls. Or they just said no."

Remembering Tom's relationship with girls, his cousin, Maureen Dobbs, daughter of Tom's beloved aunt Peg, remembered that Tom dated "some but not a lot," telling James Leonard that he had "more crushes than dates, especially crushes on Irish girls, though he thought they were above him. . . . But then he fell head over heels in love with Marge, and he's been in love with her ever since" (370).

Since he no longer had any social life due to the demands of running the business, it was inevitable that his meeting of his future wife, Margie Zybach, the woman who would change his life indelibly, would have some connection with the delivery of pizza. It was in February 1961, and Tom was delivering a pizza from the new store in

Mount Pleasant to a girls' dorm at Central Michigan University. In those days, the girls' rooms were out-of-bounds, so the switchboard operator would call the room and the customer would come down and pick up the pizza. Tom was immediately attracted to the girl at the switchboard and tried, without much success, to strike up a conversation with her while he waited for the customer to collect the pizza.

As he returned to the store, he was "on a cloud" and "really excited" by the mysterious girl he'd met. Who was she? He needed to know. Furthermore, in spite of his habitual shyness, he was determined to ask her for a date. He phoned the girl on the switchboard, told her he was the person who had just delivered the pizza, and asked her if she would like to go to a movie with him the following Monday.

The girl was indignant. "Who are you?" she asked.

Things were not going well. "I'm the guy who just delivered a pizza ten minutes ago," he repeated.

"I don't remember you," said the girl.

This was not going the way he had hoped. In desperation and in order to jog her memory, he reminded her of what he was wearing.

"Oh," she replied, "I've just come on duty." He was speaking to the wrong girl! He asked for the name of the girl who was on duty before her and was told that her name was Bonnie Hula.

Could he be put through to her room?

The switchboard operator connected her to Bonnie Hula's room and the same litany was reenacted.

"Is this Bonnie?"

"Yes."

"I'm the person who just delivered a pizza about fifteen minutes ago. Would you like to go to a movie with me next Monday?"

"Who are you?"

Once again, in a bid to jog the girl's memory and no doubt mortified by how instantly forgettable he seemed to have been, he told her what he had been wearing when he had made the delivery. At this point the girl suddenly realized the reason for the misunderstanding. She told him that she had not worked that night and that another girl had substituted for her. Tom asked for her name and was told that it was Margie Zybach. Thanking the girl, he hung up the phone and got up the nerve to phone the switch-board operator again. Could she connect him to Margie Zybach's room?

A girl answered.

"Is this Margie Zybach?"

"Yes."

Yet again he explained that he was the person who had delivered the pizza earlier. Would she like to go to a movie with him next Monday? She said that she would. Tom almost fell over in disbelief. He told her when he'd pick her up and hung up the phone. He had never felt so excited.

That Monday, Tom picked Margie up as planned and they went to see *The Guns of Navarone*, the epic World War II action-adventure film, featuring an all-star cast, including Gregory Peck, David Niven, and Anthony Quinn. The date went well, and Tom sent Margie a heart-shaped pizza for Valentine's Day, a novel romantic gesture that Margie told him had greatly impressed the girls in the dorm. On the second date, they went to see *Never on Sunday*, a Greek romantic comedy. After the movie, they proceeded to a nearby restaurant. Tom ordered a beer and Margie a wine on the rocks. "That's when it happened," Tom remembers. "I think she only drank half a glass, but she started getting a little silly, and I looked across the table at those twinkling blue eyes and that incredibly pretty face, and that was it. I was hooked." Yet it was not just the pretty face or the twinkle in the eye or the touch of silliness that so attracted him. He had known from the start that she was the right girl for him. "She was not your wild type of girl. She was a very sensible, old-fashioned, down-to-earth girl."

Thoroughly smitten, Tom resolved to propose to this girl whom he hardly knew. He went to a local jeweler and asked whether he could buy an engagement ring with no money down. He also asked whether he could return the ring if the girl to whom he meant to propose turned him down. The jeweler, whom Tom had known for a year or so because he bought papers from Tom, was very accommodating. Tom selected a half-carat diamond ring with a price tag of four hundred dollars.

On the third date with Margie, plucking up all the courage he could muster, he pulled the box with the ring in it from his pocket and handed it to her. She opened the box, looked at the ring, and was unsurprisingly rendered speechless. He asked her the million-dollar question. Would she marry him? Recovering from the initial shock, she told him that she didn't know and would need time to think about it. She agreed to take the ring while she thought things over. She would wear it when she went to bed, she told him, but wouldn't show it to her roommates.

During the following week, Tom met her every day for lunch or a snack, endeavoring to persuade the woman whom he considered his beloved to become his betrothed. By the end of the week, she had agreed to marry him. He was over the moon and must have thanked his lucky stars, or the God who made the stars, for such a transition in his life in so short a space of time. Only eighteen months earlier, he had been on skid row, homeless, penniless and defrauded of his life savings. Now, in the spring of 1961, he had a small business of his own and had found the woman of his dreams with whom his dreams for the future could be shared. Life was not only good; it could hardly be better.

CHAPTER 6

A PHOENIX RISING

TOM AND Margie were married on August 25, 1962. It was a low-key affair. Tom wore a dress suit—the only dress suit he owned—not a tuxedo, but he did go out and buy himself a new tie and a gold tie-clip for the occasion. The reception was held at his aunt Peg's house, with all the guests and a three-piece band somehow squeezing into the small living room. For the honeymoon, the married couple took the SS *Milwaukee Clipper* across Lake Michigan from Muskegon to Milwaukee and then drove up the coast to the Upper Peninsula and back down to Ann Arbor. A highlight of the honeymoon for Tom, if not perhaps for Margie, was visiting the Green Bay Packers stadium. There was nobody around, and Tom walked into the locker room and was thrilled to see the famous Number 5 jersey of Paul Hornung, the Packers' Hall of Fame running back, one of his heroes. Another highlight for the budding entrepreneur was a tour of a wax paper factory. The newlyweds were gone for a week, and before it was over, Tom had run out of cash and had to borrow money from his bride, who had saved one thousand dollars from her earnings prior to their marriage.

Life, at first, was hard. They lived in a trailer on the weekly salary of $125 that Tom paid himself. After tax, the take-home pay was only $105, and half the time, due to the precarious state of the business, he could not even cash his paychecks. In reality, therefore, the young married couple was living on a little over $50 per week. It was not much to show for the seven days a week that Tom was working to keep the pizza business going. In spite of the difficulties, Margie never complained. To supplement their income, she taught school, and they saved her paychecks. She lived very frugally, never buying things for herself, and used lots of coupons when buying groceries. They drove an old car and got by.

A little over nine months after the wedding, on May 30, 1963, their first daughter, Mary, was born, and two years later, on May 7, 1965, a second daughter, Susan, followed. By this time Margie was helping in the Ypsilanti store, answering the phone and doing the bookkeeping while the babies slept in cardboard boxes in the corner of the room. Two more daughters would follow: Margaret on August 15, 1969, the feast of the Assumption, and Barbara on August 17, 1972. Recalling the birth of their first daughter, Tom said that he'd been expecting a son purely because he had been the firstborn son of a firstborn son. He was disappointed for about ten seconds, until he set eyes on her. "When I saw her, she had an incredible smile—and she had dimples!" He remembered taking to parenthood like a fish to water—or, at least, like a father to the floor of the trailer, playing with his daughter on his hands and knees as she took her first faltering steps, holding on to the furniture as she tottered forward.

The lowest point in their marriage, which has now lasted for over half a century, was an incident that occurred shortly before Christmas in 1964. Tom had taken a group of employees out to celebrate a week of record sales and bought beer for everyone. Having a low tolerance level for alcohol, he didn't drink much himself, being content to nurse his own beer and get into the party spirit while his employees made merry. Nonetheless, he still had more than was usual, and this might have contributed to what happened when he arrived home. As he went into the bedroom, Margie rolled over and looked at him. For some reason, the questioning look in her eyes made him mad. He yelled at her, which is something he never did, and she got scared. Not knowing what he might do next, she picked up the baby to protect her. This made Tom even madder. He was lunging around clumsily and accidentally knocked over the Christmas tree, scattering ornaments and tinsel everywhere. Feeling like an idiot, he got down on his hands and knees to clean up the mess, picking up the ornaments and putting them back on the tree.

All the while, Margie sat on the couch, the baby on her lap, watching him. When he had finished, she commented sarcastically that it looked nice, which made Tom mad all over again. He knocked the tree back over in a fit of rage and, this time, jumped up and down on it like a maniac. He then stormed out, slamming the door behind him, and checked into a nearby motel. As he lay in the motel room, staring at the dark, he knew that he had just done the most stupid thing in his entire life. All night long, he fretted with feelings of shame and remorse and was overcome with fear that Margie would never forgive him.

The next morning, he went back to the trailer and helped her clear up the mess he'd made the night before, apologizing profusely for what he'd done. She was quiet for a while but finally let him kiss her, reassuring him that he was forgiven.

"I just hope you won't come home like that again," she said.

"You don't have to worry about that, honey," he replied. "I'll never have another drink the rest of my life."

For more than thirty years, he was as good as his word, never touching an alcoholic beverage of any sort. Today, he drinks wine in moderation. There is no denying that he has a will of iron. He promised Margie that he would quit smoking as soon as they were married, and the cigarette he smoked at the wedding rehearsal was his last.

Revisiting the Christmas tree episode from a distance of more than half a century, Tom is keen to insist that he was not actually drunk on the night in question and that he hardly ever drank even then. He didn't drink often, and he didn't drink much. The occasional beer or two. That was it. He might have had one beer more than usual, which would still have been only two or three, but he didn't like the effect that it had on the evening in question, and even more important, he wanted to reassure Margie that nothing of the sort would ever happen again.

In February 1965, the name of the pizza company was changed to Domino's. The idea was to use a domino for the company logo, with three dots on it to signify the three stores Tom had at the time. The initial idea was to add a dot with every new store, which, as the company expanded, was soon seen to be impractical. "Can you imagine a domino with eight thousand dots on it?" Tom would exclaim many years later.

The new name and logo coincided with a significant upturn in the company's fortunes. Throughout 1965, the business *doubled* in all three stores. The first store, the one in Ypsilanti that Tom had opened with his brother at the end of 1960, was booming. Eastern Michigan University had experienced rapid growth, which Tom believed might have had something to do with young men trying to avoid the draft during the Vietnam War, and "it seemed we literally fed the entire student body."

The upturn in fortunes ensured that Christmas 1965 was much happier than the low-point Christmas of the year before. All the heavy debt and bills accrued from the disastrous partnership with Jim Gilmore had been paid off, and Domino's could look forward to a debt-free and truly prosperous New Year. To celebrate, a Christmas party was held in the back of the Ypsilanti store. All of a sudden, there was a shout that something was on fire outside. As Tom ran outside he discovered, to his horror, that his employees had set fire to his old coat, a battered parka he had bought from J. C. Penney's years before and had worn relentlessly ever since. Then, as he looked on aghast at the flames, unable to believe his eyes, he was presented with a

new gift-wrapped coat. Apart from being a moment of fes-
tive high jinks, the act was also loaded with symbolism. The
point was that, at last, after five years of toil and struggle,
Tom could actually afford a new coat! This high-spirited
incident, which Tom still remembers as "heartwarming" all
these years later, was indicative of the family atmosphere
at Domino's in those days. As Tom lists the names of those
who worked for him in those early and heady days, he
remarks that he was best man at most of their weddings.
"They were a big part of the Domino's story. We worked
awfully hard and had a lot of fun."

No one worked harder than Tom himself, who regularly
worked from 10 a.m. till 4 o'clock the following morning,
seven days a week. But for Tom, working hard and having a lot of fun were not mutually exclusive. Nowhere was
this more in evidence than on a trip he made to New York
City in the midsixties. Tom was to be best man at the wedding in Vermont of Steve Litwhiler, an employee of Tom's
who had worked for the company since 1961 and who had
become a close friend. Since he was out east anyway, Tom
decided to check out the world's fair in New York City. He
ended up on Time Square, which, for him, was famous
because it was where all the legendary pizza places were. He
ended up in a pizza restaurant owned by an elderly Jewish
man who had been one of the pioneers of flipping pizzas
in store windows. Times were tough, the elderly proprietor
complained to his young visitor, bemoaning the fact that it
was difficult to keep good pizza makers and that they sometimes simply didn't show up for work. Sure enough, one of

his managers arrived shortly afterward to say that their best pizza maker had not come in that evening.

"I'll take his place," said Tom.

The old man looked at him in disbelief. Surely he was joking. Assuring him that he was deadly earnest, Tom said that he would work for nothing, just for the experience of making pizzas on Time Square. The old man shrugged and smiled. As good as his word, Tom worked a full eight-hour shift. "I literally stopped traffic," he remembers. "I flipped pizzas like crazy while people gathered around the window and gaped. What a night!"

Tom's obsession with pizza, present so quixotically in the Time Square episode, was evident more prosaically in the way that he continued to work incredibly long hours, seven days a week. Eventually, however, the pace of life was beginning to wear him down, and he felt the need to ease up a little, not least because he and Margie now had two daughters who also needed his time and attention. He decided to close his stores on Mondays and give himself Mondays off. Even then, however, the manner in which he spent his days off reflected his passion for pizza, or at least his determination to be the best in the business. Every Monday morning, he and Margie would load the babies into the car and head out in search of other pizza places in the Midwest. Striking out in any direction that struck their fancy, they would drive until they arrived at a town that looked interesting. They'd then check the local yellow pages for the addresses of all the pizzerias in town. They'd visit each one and talk to their owners about their business. Tom would learn valuable lessons from the owners of these stores, offering helpful tips from his own experience in return. Over a period of three years, he and Margie visited hundreds of pizzerias. Margie would sit in the car with Mary and Susie while her husband went in and checked the place out. For many years, the nearest thing that Tom and Margie had to a vacation was their annual visit to the big restaurant tradeshow in Chicago. There was, it seemed, for Margie and the children, no escape from pizza. There were only three days each year that were absolutely sacrosanct, when pizza was never on the menu, either literally or as a topic of conversation, and that was Thanksgiving, Christmas and Easter. It says much for the strength of the Monaghans' marriage that nobody seemed to mind.

As Domino's continued to prosper, and with their two girls getting bigger by the day, Tom and Margie were finally able, in 1967, to move out of the trailer in which they'd lived since their marriage and into a small three-bedroom brick ranch house between Ann Arbor and Ypsilanti. It had no basement, which was a disappointment, but big trees in the yard, which Tom particularly appreciated, and Margie was just relieved to get the children out of the claustrophobic confines of the trailer. During all those years, she had never complained. At last, after years of hard work, the Monaghans were beginning to feel that they had achieved an element of financial security.

But then disaster struck.

On February 8, 1968, Tom received a phone call at 3 a.m. to tell him that his main store, the one in Ypsilanti, was on fire. Arriving at the scene at breakneck speed, he found smoke pouring from the building and several fire engines stationed around it. At first it didn't look too bad. There seemed to be lots of smoke but no sign of fire, but as Tom was getting out of his car, a sheet of flame shot up the side of the building. After the firemen began to get the blaze under control and the flames had subsided, Tom could see large holes in the building and water dripping through. He felt sick to the stomach and utterly weak and helpless as he thought of all the things in the building that were irretrievably lost. It was as though all that he had worked so hard to build was quite literally going up in smoke.

After the dust settled on the gutted building and the full cost of the damage was assessed, it became clear that the fire would cost the company almost $150,000, a huge sum of money in 1968, and to make matters much worse, most of it would not be covered by insurance. Lesser men would have buckled under the strain of such a seemingly insurmountable disaster, but it is at times of crisis such as this that Monaghan's true mettle shines forth. On that very morning, after a sleepless night, he gathered all the key people together and worked out a plan of action. Offices were relocated while the gutted remnants of the old offices were repaired, and the pizzeria itself, which had only suffered smoke damage, was reopened within a week. Within six months, against all odds, Domino's had recouped the entire loss and had risen, phoenix-like, from the ashes of the disaster.

Ten months later, the company was stronger than ever. "New Year's 1969 was one of the happiest of my life," Tom recalled. "I was being hailed as the boy wonder of Ypsilanti's business community. Domino's had risen from its ashes. We seemed to have gained strength from the hardships of the fire. Our goal was to open a new store each week, and we were attaining it, week after week. We now had dozens of stores operating, and a dozen more were in various stages of development."

In spite of the disaster of a few months earlier, Domino's was not only growing and growing fast, but the rate of growth was accelerating. There seemed nothing that the pizza entrepreneur, Tom Monaghan, could not achieve. Indeed, less than a year after he had seen his main offices go up in flames, potentially foredooming Domino's to financial disaster and imminent collapse, he was already visualizing and projecting Domino's locations all across the country. In every sense of the word, Domino's was indeed a phoenix rising.

CHAPTER 7

THROUGH ADVERSITY
TO THE STARS

Per Ardua ad Astra
Through Adversity to the Stars

Motto of the Royal Air Force

A S THE 1960s drew to a close, Tom had every reason to be contented. He had a happy marriage and a
healthy business, and the troubled years of his childhood
and youth were becoming dim and distant memories. He
was, however, not as devout in his spiritual life as he felt he
should be, especially as he knew that spiritual health was
the most important in terms of the pecking order of priorities that he tried to live by. Looking back on the early years
of his marriage, he described himself as being "a minimal
Catholic." He did the least that was required but not much
more, even though his conscience was always niggling him
that he was not practicing his faith as he should be. He
always intended to go to confession every month, whereas
in reality, he went only about three times a year. He always
went to Mass on Sunday, "but it seems I was deathly afraid

to get there early." He was usually late, causing Margie to complain about his tardiness. "She put a lot more importance on it than I did." In short, looking back on this period, Tom reproached himself for failing to set a good example as a Catholic in the early years of his marriage.

The faith was practiced at home. Grace was always said before the early evening meal and, when he was home, Tom would always pray with the children before putting them to bed. He insisted on sending their daughters to a Catholic school, although Margie complained that the quality of the education was not very good and did not warrant the high cost they were paying for it, especially as they did not have much money in those days. In hindsight, Tom came to agree with his wife's low opinion of the so-called Catholic education that his daughters were getting. "What I found out too late was that the Catholic formation in that school was nonexistent, and as far as the faith goes, the girls would probably have been better off in the public schools." He had assumed that the Catholic schools would offer the same spiritual formation that he had received as a child, whereas in fact, the school to which his own children went actually undermined their faith. It's no wonder that, in later years, Tom became so passionate about the restoration and resurrection of genuine Catholic education.

It was, however, not only the spiritual side of Tom's life that left something to be desired. Domino's was also struggling in 1969 compared to the astronomical success of the previous year. The reason for the dramatic downturn in fortunes was the fast-track expansion of Domino's stores in residential locations. Unlike the stores in academic locations, the new residential stores were doing very poorly. Exacerbating the problem of lower sales in the residential locations was the higher cost of advertising. "On a college campus, we had what amounted to a captive audience. The students read the campus publications, so it was easy and relatively inexpensive to reach them with our advertising." Furthermore, a college community was such a closed-in phenomenon that the best advertising was word of mouth, which could spread like the proverbial wildfire and was completely free of charge. "Appealing to the general public was a completely different ball game," Tom remembers. "We had to put our ads in larger papers that charged higher rates and weren't as well targeted to our potential customers."

During the first ten months of 1969, Domino's opened thirty-two new stores, most of them in residential neighborhoods, and all but a handful of them were losing money. The euphoric and meteoric rise from the ashes that had characterized the previous year was threatening to become a catastrophic and equally meteoric fall to earth twelve months later. To make matters worse, the company's controller made a huge error in the amount of withholding taxes that the company sent in one quarter. He was off by one digit—he sent in four thousand dollars when the amount owed was forty thousand dollars—and the error wasn't discovered until three months later, by which time the next quarter's payment was due. Unable to make the payment, Domino's was hit with penalties and interest on the penalties, falling further and further behind in its payments.

The feeling of glum despondency that Tom felt at Christmastime 1969 could not have been more different from the optimistic spirit that had fueled the previous year's festivities. Although the Christian world was preparing to celebrate the birth of the Savior, it was bleak midwinter in Tom's heart. He didn't want to hold a Christmas party for his employees. He even found himself feeling resentful that all the college students had gone home for the Christmas holidays, thereby causing the usual seasonal downturn in sales. "I felt like Scrooge," Tom says, recalling his season of discontent.

In the end, one of Domino's senior employees hosted a company Christmas party in his own home. Tom went but didn't enjoy it at all. It was as though Christmas had been cancelled in Tom's heart, overburdened as it was by his fears for the future. "I felt numb," he says.

The new decade began unpromisingly. The IRS was still hounding Tom, forcing him, for the first time and against his better judgment, to sell some of his stock in the company. At the same time that the IRS was baying at his heels, he had a host of new stores that were losing money. "It was like being in quicksand," he says. "There was simply no way to stay above it." Drastic measures were needed. He closed stores and laid off some of his employees. "I detested these moves, but there was no alternative."

Sitting at his desk for several days, Tom tried to figure out exactly how much he was in debt. It was not easy because the CPA firm had quit because he couldn't pay them. Eventually he came up with a figure of $1.5 million. "I was a reverse millionaire! It was humiliating." He was

soon to discover the true meaning of the word "humili-
ation" when he received a phone call from the president
of the Ypsilanti bank, to which he was in debt to the
tune of eighty thousand dollars. Tom endeavored to make
some excuse for his unavailability, only to be showered
with abuse and told to get his "worthless carcass" to the
president's office immediately. Oh, how the mighty entrepreneur had fallen! "In one short year," Tom reflected, "the
boy wonder of Ypsilanti had become the village idiot."

At the bank's behest, Tom lost control of Domino's on
May 1, 1970, assigning all of his remaining stock to a troubleshooter whom the bank had assigned to save the company from bankruptcy. Although Tom would retain the
nominal title of company president, he would be rendered
powerless, with no authority to make executive decisions.
He would remain on his present salary of two hundred dollars per week. Tom didn't like the arrangement, but he was
now getting used to eating humble pie, and as he put it, "I
figured that part of something is better than all of nothing."

Returning home, he told Margie of his new impotent
status and received from her the customary sympathetic
understanding and a promise that they would continue to
get by. When he told her that he would still be receiving his
weekly pay check of two hundred dollars, she laughed and
said, "Oh good!" She had already "deposited" about twenty
of his salary checks into a drawer, uncashed, because they
were worthless. Her humor in such circumstances was
refreshing, even if it was gallows humor, and the sound
of her laughter in the face of adversity lightened the load
on Tom's shoulders. One recalls Chesterton's quip that

angels can fly because they take themselves lightly, whereas the devil falls by the force of his own gravity, taking himself too seriously. At this grim moment in their married life together, Margie must have seldom seemed more angelic. There she was, the mother of their two daughters, and with a third in the womb, laughing in the face of adversity and, by extension, laughing in the face of the old adversary, the devil himself, who sought to turn every adversity into despair. In her face, and in the faces of his daughters, Tom could still see a glimpse of heaven, even in the midst of his present purgatory, and as for the devil and the temptation to despair, he and it could go to hell!

The arrangement with the troubleshooter was not altogether successful, though it did ward off the imminent threat of bankruptcy, and on March 22, 1971, the company was placed once more in Tom's control. "They thought it was hopeless. They took anything of value out and gave me the company back. I was thrilled. I didn't care how long it took; I would bring the company back to solvency and from there proceed to build a national company." Few others at the time shared his optimism or his faith in the future. Everyone assumed that Domino's was still going bankrupt and that Tom's being put back at the helm was only because the temporary crew had abandoned the sinking ship. Not that Tom was unrealistic about the serious plight the company was in. "Our reputation was totally shot. There were many creditors who hadn't been paid for several years. It was difficult for our employees to cash checks. I paid about seven hundred dollars per month in bad check fees." And yet, in spite of these apparently insurmountable obstacles,

Tom described himself as being "excited to put the pieces back together." It is this uncanny ability to save the apparently sinking ship, to escape from the seemingly hopeless situation, that is the hallmark of Tom's business career. It's not the mistakes that he's made, and he has made many, but the amazing way that he has survived the mistakes and thrived in their aftermath, passing through adversity after adversity in his quest for the stars, which characterizes his life and is the secret of his success. There are few who could escape from as many impossible situations as this veritable Houdini of the business world and few who could keep their heads so well in a crisis.

And there was no doubt that Tom was now in the midst of a crisis. He managed to convince his creditors that they needed to give him more time to turn things around, but he was shocked when his own franchisees turned on him, filing a class action antitrust lawsuit against him and ceasing to pay him the royalties stipulated in their agreement. Tom realized that this lawsuit was quite literally a matter of life and death for Domino's. He arranged to meet the best antitrust attorney in Michigan and drove to Detroit for the scheduled appointment. On the way, feeling overcome with anxiety, he noticed a Franciscan monastery and pulled the car over. Going into the chapel, he knelt, prayed, and wept. Over the following months, he somehow managed to save Domino's. "During the day, I was bobbing and weaving like Muhammad Ali doing his rope-a-dope to escape the onslaught of creditors. My hands were numb from clenching my fists so hard during those endless explanations. But

at night, I was out visiting stores all over Michigan and
Ohio, and I mean seven nights a week."

Taking stock of the situation in January 1972, by
which time it was clear that disaster had been averted,
he vowed that lessons would have to be learned from the
disastrous two years that he'd just experienced. Never again
would there be expansion for expansion's sake, growing too
quickly in pursuit of fast-track growth for its own sake;
never again would untrained managers be sent into stores,
unprepared for the trials that awaited them; and never again
would he allow the company's head office to be overstaffed
and the company's modus operandi to be bogged down
with bureaucracy. Thus, leaner and fitter, Domino's moved
forward into a new year full of renewed promise. A year
later, the financial situation had improved sufficiently for
the beginning of the long process of paying back creditors,
many of whom were Tom's personal friends who'd probably expected never to see the money they were owed being
repaid. In early 1973, Tom launched Operation Surprise,
which set out a schedule whereby creditors were repaid in
monthly checks to the value of between 2 and 4 percent of
the money owed to them, a process that would continue
until all debts were erased.

With the company now expanding once again—and
on a more solid footing, the lessons of earlier mistakes having been learned—and with creditors now being paid, Tom
felt confident enough to buy a house for a little under one
hundred thousand dollars in the prestigious Barton Hills
area on the edge of Ann Arbor. It was on a scenic wooded
lot of two acres, overlooking a pond, and most important,

it had the look of something that his hero, Frank Lloyd Wright, might have designed. It was, he told Margie, their "dream house." She was less impressed. She was worried about the size of the mortgage on such an expensive property and didn't like Tom's attitude. He was too proud, preening himself with the purchase of a home in such an exclusive part of town. He invited people over just so that he could show them around the home. He had arrived. He was a success. Margie, more down-to-earth, with her feet firmly planted, had no need for such shows of peacock pride. In fact, Tom recalls that she seemed happier when they were living in trailers and struggling to make ends meet. "That's the amazing thing about my wife. She never wanted to keep up with the Joneses. She is totally unconcerned about what people think about her as far as how much money she has, how many things she has." He says that he has never heard her say that she'd like to have this or she'd like to have that. She couldn't care less about cars, one of Tom's fixations. "Her car's a car," he says. "I bought all her cars for her. She drives a car until the wheels fall off." Tom describes Margie, evidently meaning it as a great compliment to the woman he loves, as "such an ordinary, down-to-earth woman," completely unassuming, who is never happier than when shopping at Kroger. "I think it's a very noble, a great thing about her. She's remarkable." Considering Tom's hankering for the finer things in life and for the trappings of opulence, one can't help but wonder at the manifold ways that opposites attract.

Was it something paradoxical at the heart of Tom's character, or perhaps something flatly contradictory, that he could be a lifelong practicing Catholic on the one hand and yet also, and simultaneously, have so much pride in the buying of a home in a prestigious suburban neighborhood? Was there a conflict between what constituted success in the spiritual life and the sort of worldly success that Tom obviously courted, and the material trappings that went with it? Was it paradoxical in the sense that the apparent contradictions pointed to a deeper truth or was it flatly contradictory in the sense that the two visions of success were mutually exclusive and to seek both was to force oneself to live a lie, in the Orwellian sense of practicing doublethink, and therefore to be the sort of hypocrite that Christ was so vociferous in condemning? This, one might venture to suggest, is one of the great riddles at the heart of this most beguiling of men, and a riddle that must be solved, or at least pondered, if we are to understand him on anything other than the superficial level.

Something of this paradox, or contradiction, was evident in Tom's reaction to a book he read on a return flight from New York to Detroit at around the time he was purchasing the new home in Barton Hills. The book was entitled *Try Giving Yourself Away* by David Dunn and extolled the virtue of magnanimity through a life of generous giving of oneself to others. Its defining credo is summed up in this brief quote from the book: "The secret of successfully giving yourself away lies not so much in calculated actions as in cultivating friendly, warm-hearted impulses. You have to train yourself to obey giving impulses on the instant—before they get a chance to cool. When you give impulsively, something happens inside of you that makes you glow, sometimes for hours."

Practicing what Dunn preached, Tom bought a hundred copies of the book to give to all the Domino's employees and franchisees who attended the company's annual conference in 1973. He also invited Dunn to speak at the conference, but the author was unavailable on the date in question. Inspired by what he'd read in the book, Tom decided, in Dunn's absence, to speak on the book himself, making this the topic of his own address to the conference. What Dunn had learned, Tom explained to the assembled employees and franchisees, was that he was raised to believe that life was a process of *getting*, whereas he'd discovered that he was much happier when he was *giving*. Continuing, Tom referred to Dunn's "important discovery that anything which makes one glow with pleasure is beyond money calculation in this humdrum world where there is too much grubbing and too little glowing." Whereas almost anything could be bought for money, the warm impulses of the human heart could not be bought but only *given*. Furthermore, echoing the Gospel, Dunn insisted that giving to become known as generous or self-sacrificing is not giving at all but only selfishness in disguise, which serves to poison the spirit. This concept, when he had read it, had "fascinated" Tom.

Significantly, Tom held up his own wife, Margie, as a fine example of the spirit of "giving herself away" that Dunn had espoused. She had endured the long and unconventional hours Tom had worked to build Domino's and had gone without any sort of real vacation for year after year, always giving herself freely and cheerfully as a wife and mother. Then, in a candid admission of his wife's crucial role as the indispensable and powerful silence in his life, he confessed that he would never have gotten back on his feet during the recent crisis and "crash" in Domino's fortunes if it hadn't been for her.

On a purely practical level, Tom was attracted to Dunn's ideas because they represented a means of applying Christian philosophy, in a nonthreatening, nondenominational way, to the day-to-day business of Domino's. He told those attending the conference that practical applications of Dunn's ideas might include seeking ways to give more service to customers than they were expecting, or helping coworkers, or showing appreciation to suppliers for a job well done. "It underscored my own belief," Tom wrote, "that we enrich ourselves most in life when we *give* ourselves most fully and freely."

Although Dunn's ideas had exerted a powerful influence, a chance snapshot taken at the conference of Tom sitting by the pool in his swim trunks was destined to have an even longer-lasting impact. Seeing the photograph, he was shocked and dismayed to see how much weight he'd put on and horrified by the spare tire he now sported around his middle. He had stopped working out for about a year due to a shoulder injury and could not believe how out of shape he'd become. Weighing himself, he discovered that he had ballooned to two hundred pounds, about fifty pounds above his optimum weight. The shock of that photograph took him back to the rigorous exercise routine developed by the Royal Canadian Air Force that had served him well in the past. He would never look back. The RCAF program would take him eleven vigorous, merciless minutes, and he would find time to do it every day, regardless of how busy he was, for years on end. Today, forty-three years later, he still works out daily. He developed the habit of running six days a week and working out with weights at least twice a week. Ever since that day, he has weighed himself every day and kept a careful track of his daily calorie intake. "Although some people think I am too fanatic about exercise and diet," he wrote years later, "they're habits I don't want to break, because when I'm in shape, I feel better and work better." He might also have added that *physical* health was one of the important priorities that he had listed as being necessary to living a good and happy life. The top of that list of priorities was *spiritual* health, an area in which he was also making progress, having begun, during the dark days of the "crash," to attend Mass daily and not merely weekly.

As for *financial* health, the last and least important in the list of priorities that he tried to live by, things had never been better. By the end of 1973, Domino's had seventy-six stores in thirteen states. Profit was relatively modest, at $130,000 for the year, but in Tom's words, it was "very gratifying after our long immersion in red ink." As another year had come to an end, the most successful yet, he might have gained encouragement from the motto of the Royal Air Force, whose fitness regimen he was now following: *Per Ardua ad Astra.* Through Adversity to the Stars!

CHAPTER 8

SPLURGING AND SUBSIDIARITY

TOM REALIZED that Domino's had made the big time when he received a phone call from Frank Carney, chairman of Pizza Hut, requesting a meeting to discuss a possible takeover. Tom told Carney that he didn't think that any offer would persuade him to sell, but he agreed to meet him. He was flattered that his rising star, still relatively small but in the ascendant, had attracted the interest of the owner of the largest pizza chain in the world. Tom told Carney that he felt as though Raquel Welch, probably the most celebrated Hollywood sex symbol of the time, had asked him for a date. He was "tempted and flattered" but his "marriage vows" would make him turn the offer down. Carney flew to Ypsilanti for the meeting but, as promised, Tom refused to be persuaded to sell, however seductive the offer. He was nonetheless pleased to have met Carney, because some of the things his competitor told him had helped to confirm his own strong faith in the Domino's concept.

Toward the end of 1974, Domino's attracted the attention of another giant corporation, though this time the
attention was anything but welcome. Amstar Corporation,
owner of Domino Sugar, sued Domino's for trademark
infringement. It took years for the case to actually come
to court, and when the trial finally opened on January 15,
1979, it dragged on for months. The legal costs accrued
by both companies were huge, and the potential further
cost to Domino's, were the company to lose and be forced
to change its name, would be astronomical. Tom and his
attorneys were, however, confident of victory. Eventually,
on September 11, the judge delivered his verdict, which, to
Tom's surprise and horror, was in Amstar's favor. It was a
devastating blow. Tom decided to appeal even though it was
unusual for a case of this sort to be overturned on appeal,
and to make matters worse, the judge ruled that Domino's
could not open any more stores under the Domino's name
during the appeal process. Forced to come up with a new
name for its new stores, at least temporarily, forty new outlets were opened during the appeal process with the name
Pizza Dispatch.

On April 10, 1980, Tom arrived at work to find his
staff acting far more boisterously than usual. Jokingly, he
asked them what was going on and reminded them that
they had work to do. Someone told him that they had
won the lawsuit on appeal. It didn't register. Again he said,
still humorously, that there was work to do. "Tom," someone said, "we won the lawsuit." Then it registered. Margie was among the boisterous group. He grabbed her arm
and led her into his office, closed the door, sat down with

her on the couch, hugged her, and then cried like a baby for about ten minutes. Then, recovering his composure, he ordered champagne and informed everyone that it was time to celebrate.

Amstar appealed to the US Supreme Court but, after a further six months of worry, the Supreme Court justices rejected the appeal, bringing the case to an end. "It was finally over," Tom said, "we won!" It had been, he added, "six years of hell."

Although one can certainly understand why Tom could describe the high anxiety that the court case must have caused as "hell," and though, no doubt, the fear of defeat in the lawsuit must have cast something of a gloomy shadow over the company during the six years that the case dragged on, one suspects that the company's growth might have been maintained had it not been for the near-disastrous role that a senior executive played, whom Tom had employed in December 1974. Russell Hughes was a micromanager and centralizer of power who refused to put any real power of initiative in the hands of his subordinates. "Hughes felt he had to understand every action thoroughly before he'd make a move," Tom wrote. "He belabored even the smallest decision." Tom was especially concerned about the restrictive policies that Hughes had introduced governing the opening of new stores, the practical consequence of which was that the company had stopped growing altogether by the end of 1975. Things got even worse in 1976, and Tom could hardly believe it when Hughes informed him that his plan was to get rid of the franchisees and have corporate stores only, further proof of Hughes's power-centralist

approach and his obsession with centralized micromanagement. The final straw was Hughes's egocentric "offer"
to take over the whole company, buying Tom out as
part of a leveraged package. Tom responded by asking
Hughes to resign.

Tom described the two years that followed Hughes's
departure as "Domino's coming-of-age." With the prospect
of the Amstar trial looming ominously in the background,
and the huge expenditure of time, energy and money that
it demanded, Tom set about rebuilding the company in
the wake of Hughes's mismanagement. Reversing Hughes's
management strategy, Tom set about revitalizing the company's relationship with its franchisees and reenergizing the
strategy for opening new stores. He introduced a sponsorship program that rewarded franchises for giving up their
top managers so that the best managers could become franchisees in their own right. This incentive-driven initiative
became the main growth vehicle for the company during
the heady eighties and was nothing less than a stroke of
genius on Tom's part. Practicing the axiom that he was
always preaching, that "people are not machines," he
was careful to look after the corporate store managers as
well as the franchisees, rewarding them with 25 percent of
the profits of their store. Wishing to free as many of his
employees as possible from what a Chestertonian distributist
might call the proletarianized status of wage slavery, Tom
also initiated an internal financing system enabling hundreds of Domino's workers who had few assets and could
not therefore borrow from banks or finance companies to

become franchisees and therefore get into business in their own right.

On September 10, 1977, Domino's finally became debt-free, all the creditors from the "crash" of 1969 having been repaid. The new debt-free status enabled the company to move its corporate headquarters to Ann Arbor, thereby bidding adieu to the haphazard collection of lean-to buildings and Quonset huts that had served as the company's headquarters in Ypsilanti for so many years. Tom described the new headquarters as "the first presentable office we'd had since I'd been in business."

With the new levels of opulence, Tom became more of a showman in the way that he shared the company's wealth, giving away expensive watches as incentives to his franchisees. This began in 1977 when he awarded a Bulova watch with a Domino's logo on its face to a franchisee who had achieved a twenty-thousand-dollar sales week. This established a tradition that became more extravagant as the years went by. For the next few years, he gave away Seiko watches and, after that, hundreds of eight-hundred-dollar Rolex watches. He also developed increasingly expensive habits with regard to his own personal taste in watches, buying a five-thousand-dollar solid-gold Swiss Patek Philippe used from a friend in 1979. It was all a long way from the years of struggle or the "crash" of 1969, which had left him as what he called a "reverse millionaire," owing $1.5 million, and with the humiliating prospect of bankruptcy looming.

Domino's opened its two-hundredth store in November 1978, another significant milestone in the company's seemingly inexorable ascendency. Exuding confidence, Tom told a meeting of the Ann Arbor President's Club in 1980 that his five-year goal was to make Domino's Pizza a household name in America. "Eyebrows shot up like window shades all around the room," Tom recalled. "I heard loud groans of protest and a few snickers. I couldn't blame the members for being skeptical. Most of them knew that Domino's, with 290 stores, was pretty small change in the franchising field." Furthermore, several of the members were well aware that Domino's had recently lost the lawsuit that Amstar Corporation had brought. Although Domino's had appealed the decision, few expected the appeal to be successful. It seemed reasonable to assume that the court-imposed name change would cause a confusion of corporate identity, the necessity to advertise heavily to make the new name known, and a significant loss of revenue. It was little surprise that the members of the Club did not take Tom's claims seriously. After the meeting, one member approached him and scoffed at the preposterous nature of his goal. "A household word, eh? You've got to be kidding, Monaghan."

Tom responded that he was not "kidding." He predicted that the present rate of the company's growth, 40 to 50 percent a year, would be maintained and that, in consequence, Domino's would have at least two thousand stores by 1985, which would make it truly a national company with nationwide recognition. True to his word, by the time that Domino's celebrated its twenty-fifth anniversary in December 1985, the company had 2,600 stores, spread across all fifty states and with a presence in six other countries. By the same year, according to an independent survey, 90 percent of the American population recognized the name Domino's Pizza.

In the summer of 1980, awash with confidence in his own ambitions, Tom met one of his all-time heroes during a family vacation in Southern California. He had tried for years to meet Ray Kroc, the man who had built McDonald's into the most successful fast-food empire in the world. As early as 1968, Tom had written to the McDonald's corporate headquarters, hoping to meet the man whom he described as his idol. His request was refused. From 1972 onward, undeterred by continued rebuttals and unprepared to take "no" for an answer, he had someone call Kroc's office in San Diego once a month to try to arrange the elusive meeting. Then, during the family vacation, while Margie and the girls were visiting Sea World and the San Diego Zoo, Tom finally got to meet his hero.

After being kept waiting in the lobby for what seemed an eternity and fearing that it meant that the meeting would be cancelled, he was finally ushered into the presence of the Emperor of Fast Food. Tom approached Kroc, like any self-respecting fan, with a dog-eared copy of his idol's autobiography, which was duly autographed for him. Tom had hoped to learn from Kroc, whose precepts he had underlined throughout the length of Kroc's book, but the McDonald's founder seemed more interested in learning about Domino's. "There was something intriguing about him," Tom remembers. "He was famous for being a great listener. I had a kind of a unique concept, not only the business itself, but the way I did business, and he picked up on it right away. I've never seen anybody so quick to understand what I was saying. It was delightful!"

The meeting had been scheduled to last only fifteen minutes, but the two entrepreneurs chatted for two and a half hours, the seventy-eight-year-old founder of McDonald's seeming to relish the company of his forty-three-year-old protégé. One of the things that they discussed was Tom's dream of one day owning his beloved Detroit Tigers, thereby emulating Kroc who was, at the time, owner of the San Diego Padres. "Why would you want to do that?" Kroc asked. "Baseball is the craziest business I've ever gotten into in my life. You don't own anything! It's more frustrating than the hamburger business. If I were you, I'd forget it." Tom wasn't about to let Kroc deter him from following his dreams, preferring to dismiss Kroc's words of discouragement as a reflection of the poor way that the Padres were performing at the time and also perhaps as a reflection of Kroc's despondency over the fact that the Padres' star player, Dave Winfield, was about to join the Yankees.

That evening, while Tom was still basking in the afterglow of the audience he'd had with his hero, he received a phone call from the excited manager of the local Domino's store in San Diego. "Hey, Tom, guess what . . . Ray Kroc just came into our store and ordered a pizza!" Tom was overjoyed. "I guess I must have made some sort of impression on him," he thought. Whether Kroc's decision to patronize one of Tom's stores was a genuine mark of respect for the kindred spirit he'd met that day or whether he was simply checking on the competition out of curiosity or both, the gesture was enough to make Tom's day, and not simply his day but his vacation. It was not so much the icing on the cake as the topping on the pizza.

Once again, one is perplexed by the paradox or contradiction at the heart of the man who is Monaghan. On the one hand, there is the Catholic who by this time is going to daily Mass, trying to put his Christian faith at the center of his life, and trying to put the dignity of the human person at the center of his business strategy; on the other is the man who is buying five-thousand-dollar watches and who idolizes business leaders, such as Ray Kroc, who have a reputation for ruthlessness. Even in those days, writing in the mideighties, Tom seemed well aware of the problem, lamenting the unethical nature of much business competition and criticizing Kroc himself for sanctioning unethical business practices: "More often than not, the attitude toward direct competitors is the one expressed by Ray Kroc: 'It's rat eat rat, dog eat dog. I'll kill 'em . . . I'm going to kill 'em before they kill me.' Much as I admire Kroc, I don't share that philosophy."

Another passion that Tom could now indulge was his lifelong love for architecture and especially his passion for the work of Frank Lloyd Wright. In late 1980, he employed the services of Larry Brink, an architect who had been trained by Wright, to help him make grandiose alterations to the family home in Barton Hills that he had bought seven years earlier. As usual, Margie had helped to keep Tom's feet on the ground, refusing to let him do any work on the house until they could pay in cash, but now that Domino's had won the Amstar suit, and with Tom full of the confidence about Domino's future of which he had boasted earlier in the year at the Ann Arbor President's Club, it seemed the right time to move forward with his ambitious plans for their home. Soon the plans that he and Brink had for the house outgrew the house itself in terms of the sheer scale and opulence of what they envisioned. The proposed remodeling would have cost about two million dollars, much more than the house had cost to buy, but complaints from community officials, and their restrictions on what they would permit to be built, forced Tom to abandon further construction before many of his and Brink's plans could be brought to fruition. Margie was not as disappointed as her husband by the enforced change of plans. She had always been less than keen on the huge scale of the planned alterations, being much happier than Tom to live in relative simplicity.

In spite of Tom's developing habit of spending lavishly on his passions and enthusiasms, a tendency to "splurge" that would become more marked in the years ahead, his level-headed ability to lead Domino's, whether in a crisis or during periods of unprecedented success, was nothing less than astonishing. Don Vlcek (pronounced "Volcheck"), whom Tom hired in the late seventies and who would become one of Domino's longest serving executives, offered a priceless glimpse into Tom's leadership skills in conversation with James Leonard. "He was always there to celebrate and always there for a crisis, but the rest of the time he got out of people's hair and let them figure out how to reach the goal without telling them how to do it. He told me what to do maybe twice in all the years I worked for him" (93). This way of doing things, or modus operandi, was indicative of the trust that Tom retained in the dignity of the human person in spite of that trust having been betrayed on more than one occasion in the past, a trust that was itself a reflection of the teaching of the Catholic Church that he had always espoused.

In stark contrast to the micromanagement and obsessive centralism of Russell Hughes, Tom trusted his employees to take responsibility for their own actions:

> I believe in giving people responsibility, and I insist on letting them make their own mistakes. This practice isn't abdication, and it isn't really delegation, either. It's the difference between a coach who lets the quarterback be the field general and one who calls all the plays from the sidelines. I believe in picking the right quarterback and letting him do it himself. I guess I tend to trust people more than others do. In baseball, I like to see a guy go all out and dive for the ball. If he misses, I say, "Nice try." The same thing applies in Domino's. I want my people to go all out. They'll make mistakes that way, but there's nothing wrong with making a mistake, providing you learn from it.

This management philosophy, rooted in "trusting the quarterbacks," led to Tom's decision to decentralize Domino's in 1981, a change in corporate strategy that contributed significantly to the explosive growth that followed. At first, there were six regions, each named after the regional director or "quarterback" responsible for running them. Within a few years, the ongoing decentralization would lead to the formation of seven more regions. This regional system had the desired result of leading to "rapid but well-orchestrated growth." "Decentralization had a positive effect in corporate headquarters too," Tom reported. "It reduced bureaucracy and freed me to concentrate on a few key areas."

Such decentralization was also a practical application of the principle of subsidiarity at the heart of the Catholic Church's social teaching.

In the *Catechism of the Catholic Church*, subsidiarity is discussed in the context of the dangers inherent in too much power being centralized in the hands of the state: "Excessive intervention by the state can threaten personal freedom and initiative. The teaching of the Church has elaborated the principle of subsidiarity, according to which a community of a higher order should not interfere in the internal life of a community of a lower order, depriving the latter of its functions, but rather should support it in case of need and help to co-ordinate its activity with the activities of the rest of society, always with a view to the common good" (CCC 1883). Put simply, the principle of subsidiarity rests on the assumption that the rights of small communities (e.g., families or neighborhoods), should not be violated by the intervention of larger communities (e.g., the state or centralized bureaucracies). Thus, for instance, in practical terms, the rights of parents to educate their children without the imposition by the state of "politically correct" school curricula would be enshrined by the principle of subsidiarity. Parental influence in schools is subsidiarist; state influence is antisubsidiarist.

This is all very well, it might be argued, but subsidiarity is only applicable to the world of politics and not to the world of economics. The great economist and Catholic convert E. F. Schumacher would beg to differ, advocating a way of running businesses not that dissimilar to the way that Tom Monaghan was running Domino's. Schumacher developed a theory of large-scale organization that aimed at employing the principle of subsidiarity within the structure of the largest businesses, what might be called "smallness within bigness." This principle stipulates that it is wrong to assign to higher levels in the organization those functions that can be carried out lower down.

Schumacher based this aspect of his theory on the "principle of subsidiary function" promulgated by Pope Pius XI in his encyclical *Quadragesimo Anno*: "It is an injustice and at the same time a grave evil and disturbance of right order to assign to a greater and higher association what lesser and subordinate organizations can do." Although the Pope had intended this principle to be applicable to society as a whole, Schumacher applied it specifically to functions within large corporations. In practical terms, this means that large organizations should consist of many semiautonomous units, which he calls "quasi-firms." Each of these should be given a great degree of freedom to offer the greatest possible encouragement to creativity and entrepreneurship. Parallels with Tom Monaghan's relationship with his own executives and also with the franchise system at the core of Domino's success are obvious.

Schumacher symbolizes this subsidiarist structure in terms of a man holding a large number of balloons in his hand. Each of the balloons has its own buoyancy and lift so that the man only has to stand beneath them, holding the strings in his hand to keep them together. Each balloon is both an administrative and an entrepreneurial unit, minimizing bureaucracy and maximizing innovation. In contrast, the CEO of a large corporation who insists on micromanagement, failing to give his subordinates the freedom they need to operate efficiently, could be likened to a juggler. Since everything depends on the ability of one man to juggle, he is more likely to drop the balls when more are added—that is, the larger the organization, the less likely that the all-powerful center will be able to manage its component parts efficiently.

Tom Monaghan, never having made a study of Schumacher's international bestseller *Small is Beautiful*, published in 1973, nor of the papal documents that were a large part of Schumacher's inspiration, had arrived at similar conclusions from a combination of common sense and the learning of lessons from mistakes he had made. In putting these principles into his business practices, he was living in accordance with the teachings of the Church, even if his tendency to splurge on personal possessions and personal passions might seem to violate the spirit of the Gospel. Tom Monaghan was, therefore, like so many other people, a paradox personified or, perhaps, and worse, a walking contradiction.

CHAPTER 9

PIZZA TIGER

A S THE positive impact of Tom's subsidiarist restruc-
turing of Domino's began to pay dividends, he spoke
confidently of his hopes and expectations for the company's future. In an article published in *The Ann Arbor
Observer* in 1982, which Leonard quotes in his biography,
he declared that he expected Domino's to have nine hundred outlets by the end of that year, two thousand by 1984,
and a store in every US town with a population of over
ten thousand people by 1985. It was big talk, but there
were fewer scoffers than there used to be. The fact is that
Monaghan was building a reputation as having something
of a Midas touch. With the rapid growth of Domino's at
the time, its market value was approaching $250 million.
He was no longer a "reverse millionaire," threatened with
imminent bankruptcy, but a millionaire several times over
who could reasonably expect to get considerably richer in
the years ahead. Asked for his thoughts about being so rich,
he responded unequivocally: "Money is not evil, as so many
people think. It pays for Bibles and churches and hospitals"
(99). He might also have added that it could buy major

league baseball teams, because very shortly afterward, he would stun the sporting world with his acquisition of the Detroit Tigers.

Tom had always loved sports, all sorts of sports, both as a player and as a spectator. His father had been a very good baseball player, and Tom had played baseball, football, and basketball at the orphanage, excelling especially at the last of these but enjoying all three. He had become a very good ping-pong player as a teenager in Traverse City and had played ping-pong competitively in the Marines. As a busy pizza entrepreneur and family man, he had still found time to play basketball once a week with his friends. He had also become a keen runner, having whipped himself back into shape with the Royal Canadian Air Force's fitness program, and in the autumn of 1980, he had run in the New York Marathon, recording a highly reputable time of four hours and nineteen minutes.

Prior to the running of the marathon in New York, Tom had attended a seminar, one of the speakers at which was a young businessman, Fred Wilpon, who had made his fortune in real estate and who would later lose most of it through his involvement in the Madoff investment scandal. Wilpon was the same age as Tom (actually about four months older) and was president and CEO of the New York Mets. Wilpon spoke about how his high-profile involvement with the Mets had been beneficial to his business.[*] Wilpon's testimony was a revelation to Tom and was

---

[*] James Leonard, in his biography of Monaghan, quotes Tom as saying that Wilpon had said in his speech that he had bought the Mets. In

the justification he needed for pursuing his dream of owning the Tigers, which would not only serve as a personal
wish-fulfillment but also help Domino's. Armed with the
vision of this win-win scenario, he set about trying to make
it happen.

Of all Tom's daughters, Susie, the second eldest, was
the one who shared his passion for sports. She was, Tom
claimed, nearly as big a Tigers fan as he was. As a reward
for the sixteen-year-old receiving high grades in school, he
took her, in March 1982, to visit the Tigers' spring training
camp in Lakeland, Florida. Introducing himself and Susie
to Jim Campbell, the club's president, he mentioned that
he'd be interested in buying the club if the owner, John
Earl Fetzer, was interested in selling. Fetzer shared the same
birthday as Tom, being thirty-six years older to the day, and
was only a week or so away from his eighty-fourth birthday.
Nonetheless, in spite of his advanced years, he was report-
edly not interested in selling the club that he had owned
for over twenty years.

Sometime later, unbeknownst to Tom, Campbell phoned
Fetzer to say that he might have found the right person to
take over the Tigers when Fetzer decided he wanted to sell.

On March 31, 1983, Tom returned to Lakeland for a
private meeting with Fetzer that Campbell had set up. A
further meeting followed at the Westin Hotel in Detroit on
August 25. It was the Monaghans' wedding anniversary, a
date that was normally kept sacrosanct on the calendar as

---

fact, at the time, he only owned a 1 percent stake and would not buy
the team until 2002.

a day that Tom kept clear so that he could celebrate appropriately with Margie. He had never missed his anniversary date with his wife in the previous twenty-one years, but this one year, he made an exception to the golden rule, with Margie's blessing, and went ahead with the meeting with Fetzer. The meeting went well, contracts were signed a month or so later, and Monaghan's ownership of the Detroit Tigers was made public at a press conference on October 10.

The Tigers had not come cheap. Although the price was not disclosed at the time, it was fifty-three million dollars. Dreams cost nothing, but they can be mighty expensive when they come true!

Remembering the speech that Wilpon had made three years earlier, Tom rationalized the huge expenditure on the grounds that his ownership of the Tigers would be worth at least five million dollars a year to Domino's in advertising and publicity.

The boy from the orphanage had come a long way from the days when he dreamed of one day playing shortstop for the Tigers, daydreaming about future stardom while tuning in to WIBM to listen to the play-by-play commentary of the team's games. Yet the orphanage was never far from his thoughts. Even as he was negotiating to buy the Tigers, he acknowledged the orphanage's formative influence upon him when asked to speak about the person who had influenced him most. Thinking back over his life, he realized that he owed a greater debt to Sister Berarda than to anyone else. "One thing she used to say all the time, her English was a little broken, was *'Tommy, be a good boy.'*" It was as though those words were always with him, a haunting reminder "in the back of my brain" of the moral imperatives that should govern his life, in good times and bad.

Tom decided to track down Sister Berarda, hoping she was still alive. He discovered that she was not only very much alive but still very active, running a Montessori school in Livonia, Michigan. A reunion was arranged, which Tom described as "wonderful," his voice charged with emotion. He invited her to attend the Domino's annual awards banquet at which he gave a speech acknowledging Sister Berarda's defining influence in his life, reducing his elderly mentor to joyful tears. He then showed his appreciation for her by giving a scholarship in her name to Madonna University, a scholarship that is still available at Madonna to full-time students majoring in child development.

Meanwhile, Tom's hopes that the huge price he'd paid for the Tigers might be justified by the publicity it would generate for Domino's appeared to be vindicated in the weeks and months following his buying of the team. On New Year's Day 1984, *The Detroit News* carried a full-page story emblazoned with the headline "Monaghan's Dough Stole Show: Tigers' Sale Heads List of Leading 1983 Local Sports Stories." Although it had been a successful year for the Detroit Lions, who had won their first divisional title in twenty-six years, the Lions were still being eclipsed by the Tigers. "Money eclipses success," *The Detroit News* declared, announcing that Monaghan's buying of the Tigers was voted the top local sports story of the year. The Lions' victory couldn't match Monaghan's coup. "The victories . . . don't offer the freshest recollection of the past year in Detroit sport. Rather, 1983 will go down in lore as the year a pizza tycoon bought the Tigers."

"It was said to be the biggest sports story in Detroit in ten years," Tom recalls. "The media couldn't seem to get enough of this pizza guy from Ann Arbor. I was hounded by the media. Letters and calls came in from all over the country from people I hadn't heard from in years, some from my childhood. The people in Domino's were thrilled. It really boosted the morale throughout the company."

The good publicity continued. The cover of the April 1984 edition of *Monthly Detroit* sported a full color photograph of Tom, wearing a Tigers cap and posing with a real-life Tiger. Inside the magazine, a twelve-page article waxed romantically about Tom's trials and tribulations, from his life in an orphanage to his success as a pizza tycoon. Alluding to Tom's buying of the Tigers, the article offered an intriguing psychological insight into the reasons for Tom's apparently insatiable ambition and his goal-driven lifestyle: "Achieving the goal of a lifetime doesn't end anything. It has always been goals that directed and gave direction to Tom's life. Most of the time, he says, he is thinking about where he's going to be next year. It's a habit from his childhood. When you've had no past for so many years, all you can do is look to the future."

The article then lists some of the goals that were especially motivating Tom in the spring of 1984. These included a desire to shed ten pounds in weight, a desire to learn new languages, and his plans to build a tower designed years earlier by Frank Lloyd Wright but never built. Most intriguing was the earliest mention of his hopes to start a college, a goal that would not be reached until fourteen years later. Not surprisingly, another goal was to bring success to his beloved Tigers.

Much of the spring of 1984 was spent traveling on the Tigers' team bus and making frequent visits to spring training in Lakeland, Florida. One of the perks of his new position was not only fraternizing with the current players but meeting the heroes of his childhood, not least of whom was Hoot Evers, his favorite player during the years at the orphanage. "Imagine the thrill when I flew in my jet to Lakeland and who was there to pick me up and take me to the spring training facility but Hoot Evers! He apologized to me that Jim Campbell, the president, couldn't come. I assured him that that wasn't a problem, that *he* was my favorite player as a kid."

As the season began, with the Tigers getting off to a flying start, Tom was home in bed. He had wanted to be at opening day in Minnesota but had fallen ill that day. He ran a fever of 103 degrees for four days in a row and found the sickness hard to shake, missing all but four of the Tigers' opening thirteen games, twelve of which they'd won. "I'm not complaining one bit," Tom told a reporter from *The Detroit News* in an article that appeared April 24, 1984. "If that's what happens when I get the flu, I'll catch it again."

Tom was again on the cover of a magazine in August 1984, this time of *Success*, "the magazine for achievers," sporting a Tigers cap, clutching a baseball, and beaming at the camera. The seven-page article, entitled "Pizza Tiger," described in glowing terms "How Tom Monaghan Conquered Business and Baseball."

It might have seemed in the summer of 1984 that things could not get much better for Monaghan the Conqueror. Yet, by October, the Tigers, as winners of the American League, had made it to the heady heights of the World Series, being matched against the San Diego Padres. If Ray Kroc had not died earlier in the same year, thereby ending his ten-year reign as owner of the Padres, the Tigers–Padres matchup would have been billed as the battle of the fast-food giants, McDonalds versus Domino's, Kroc versus Monaghan, the burger baron versus the pizza king. It had only been four years since Tom had been granted an audience with Kroc, sitting in awe in his hero's presence and mentioning bashfully his hopes of buying the Tigers. Now, having achieved his goal far sooner than he would have dared to hope, he was on the brink of beating Kroc's own team at the World Series. It was almost too good to be true—and yet true it was!

On October 1, a little over a week before the World Series, Tom presented a Detroit Tigers cap to US President Ronald Reagan when the latter spoke at a lunch gathering in Detroit. The two men joked with each other at the podium, with Reagan placing the Tigers cap on his head. Asked who he was rooting for in the World Series, Reagan sidestepped the question in quintessential political fashion, explaining that he was "supposed to be president of all the people." As a lifelong follower of the Chicago Cubs, the President ruefully recalled the World Series of 1945, when the Tigers had triumphed over the Cubs. If the Cubs had not narrowly lost out to the Padres by three games to two in the National League Championship Series a week earlier, the 1984 World Series could have been a repeat of the Tigers–Cubs matchup of almost half a century earlier.

The first game of the World Series was played on October 9 at Jack Murphy Stadium, home of the Padres, with the Tigers emerging triumphant. Although the Padres won the second game, the Tigers would go on to win all three games at the Tiger Stadium in Detroit, winning the series comfortably by four games to one. The celebrations following the final game on October 14 would be something that Tom would never forget and forever relish. Champagne was fizzing, flowing and spraying around the hot room. Tom, beaming in disbelief, was at the center of it. One of the players sprayed him with champagne. Another doused him with ice-cold water. Lance Parrish, who had hit a home run, danced triumphantly, his faced smeared with lipstick from countless victory kisses. Kirk Gibson, who had hit two home runs, roared like a lion, inadvertently punching his manager in the eye before dousing Tom with the ice-cold water, to the rambunctious delight of everyone present.

"That 1984 season contained enough great memories to last a lifetime," Tom remembers. "I can close my eyes and replay Jack Morris's no hitter, tremendous hits by Kirk Gibson, and great catches like the one Chet Lemon made by turning all the way around. The exhilaration I felt as champagne was poured on my head—not to mention a five-gallon bucket of ice water dumped on me by Gibson—when we won the World Series is unforgettable."

Looking back on this incredible championship-winning season, Tom is understandably proud of the team's record. "I knew they had the makings of a great team, but I had no idea they would play as they did in that incredible 1984 season. They roared into first place in the American league at the outset of the season with nine straight wins. They won thirty-five of their first forty games, the best start in baseball history. And they stayed in first place throughout the season." At the time, only six other teams in the annals of baseball had led the league wire-to-wire. The last team to do it, prior to the Tigers, was the legendary New York Yankees team of 1927, almost sixty years earlier, the year that Babe Ruth hit sixty home runs. "In team play, the 1984 Tigers outdid those storied Yankees," Tom says, "and they capped their fabulous summer by winning the World Series."

To commemorate the championship season, Tom was awarded a World Series ring. Describing it as "big and a bit gaudy," for a long time he wouldn't leave home without it. He took to wearing it on the same finger as his plain and anything-but-gaudy wedding band, enjoying the contrast. The wedding band, diminutive and humble, cost a mere twelve dollars when it had been purchased more than twenty years earlier. The World Series ring, big and brash, had cost him fifty-three million dollars—the price he had paid for the Tigers. It was not until many years later that he came to realize that the price he had paid for the Tigers did not adequately reflect the real cost to himself and his family in terms of things that money could neither buy nor measure. That truly "magical first season" would come at a considerable cost. "All this publicity and success in such a short period of time changed me, much of it negatively."

CHAPTER 10

THE DOMINO'S EFFECT

ON OCTOBER 4, 1984, three days after present-
ing President Reagan with a Tigers cap and ten days
before the Tigers won the World Series, Tom read an article in *The Wall Street Journal* about the ideas of Booker T.
Whatley, a pioneer of small-scale sustainable farming. Surprisingly, perhaps, the big and brash pizza billionaire and
pioneer of the fast-food revolution found himself positively
inspired by this black university professor from the Deep
South whose vision was proclaimed in the advice to farmers to "stay small but get smart."

Born in 1915 in rural Alabama, Whatley was raised on
a small family farm, the oldest of twelve children. Receiving a doctorate in horticulture from Rutgers University,
he became a professor of agriculture at Tuskegee University, where he developed new varieties of grapes and sweet
potatoes as well as pioneering "smaller and smarter" as an
economically sustainable strategy for small farmers. He was
an early advocate of the pick-your-own (or u-pick) direct-
marketing strategies for small farmers that is now a worldwide phenomenon.

The article that Tom picked up and read in *The Wall Street Journal* in October 1984 was published under the headline "Booker T. Whatley Contends His Program Will Help Small Farms Make Big Money." One can imagine Tom's interest being piqued by the memory of the small farms and small farmers that he had experienced as a boy, when he and his adoptive families had been forced to live in conditions of abject poverty. One can imagine also that his curiosity was aroused by Whatley's claims that such small farms and poor farmers could make "big money."

Although Tom was apparently unaware of E. F. Schumacher's international bestseller, published a decade earlier, there are striking parallels between Whatley's "smaller but smarter" and Schumacher's "small is beautiful." The article that Tom settled down to read began by setting the small, smart, and beautiful scenario:

> For too long the prevailing wisdom among small farmers has been to get big or get out, says Booker T. Whatley. His advice: Stay small but get smart.
>
> A farmer with only 25 acres can gross more than $100,000 a year, according to Mr. Whatley. But to do that, he has to start thinking less about big tractors and more about marketing.

According to the journalist writing the article, Whatley's academic and scientific credentials meant that he couldn't be simply dismissed "as just another back-to-the-land idealist." Reading on, Tom recalled feeling that Whatley's views harmonized with his own experience of farming. Whatley was "dead right" in observing that today's average small farm was nothing but a scaled-down big farm, attempting to ape the agribusiness methods advocated by the US Department of Agriculture with no real hope of competing. Having agreed with Whatley about the nature of the problem, Tom was really fired up by the purely practical aspects of Whatley's vision for small-scale agriculture: "At the heart of Mr. Whatley's ideal small farm is a 'pick-your-own' club. People who live in a nearby city pay a nominal membership fee for the right to pick fresh vegetables at a cost of 40 percent below what they would pay for the prematurely harvested produce on supermarket shelves. The pick-your-own club saves money by eliminating most harvesting costs and circumventing the middleman."

Tom recalled that reading this paragraph "made me sit up and take notice." Feeling inspired by the vision presented to him, Tom decided to set aside some of the property on Domino's Farms, the company's new corporate headquarters just outside Ann Arbor, for use as "a model of Dr. Whatley's concept for saving the small farm in America." He called Whatley's home in Montgomery, Alabama, and was told that Whatley was scheduled to give a lecture at Michigan State University. Tom made arrangements to attend the lecture and to meet with this newly discovered mentor afterward. Describing the talk as "fascinating," Tom sat riveted to every word as Whatley illustrated his points with a large chart showing his model twenty-five-acre farm. "I was completely captivated by this sixty-eight-year-old black man," Tom remembers. After the talk, Tom explained his hope that Whatley would build one of his model farms at Domino's corporate headquarters. The two became firm friends, with Tom thirty years later describing Whatley as "a delightful guy." More meetings followed, and a year later, Whatley finalized his plans for an adapted version of his model farm to be established at Domino's Farms.

Tom would write later that the main reason that he desired that Domino's headquarters should be a working farm was probably his "boyhood love of farm life," adding that his sympathy "with Frank Lloyd Wright's idea of integrating architectural forms with a rural countryside had a lot do with it, too." And yet, as he disclosed in a recent interview, part of the attraction of Whatley's vision was that it adhered to the Church's teaching that the family should be the center of the economic and social fabric of society. The type of farm that Whatley advocated would enable families to support themselves on twenty-five acres. This was subsidiarity that could be made to work in a modern economic setting, much as Tom's own decentralizing of Domino's corporate structure was a practical application of successful subsidiarist principles.

At the same time that Tom was becoming a champion of the smallness and beauty of family-owned farms, he was also advocating that "big is best" as far as Domino's Pizza was concerned. In 1985, Domino's was better known than ever, with 90 percent of the US population recognizing Domino's Pizza as a brand name. As for Tom himself, his high-profile position as owner of the all-conquering Detroit Tigers, coupled with his corporate success, had turned him into a celebrity. "For years, I had pursued success and certainly wanted to be seen as successful, especially after all the setbacks and humiliations I went through. Now I had become the paragon of success—the classic Horatio Alger story—from an orphanage to years of business struggles to a rousing success." He owned a company that pioneered and blazed a trail for the burgeoning pizza delivery business, capturing at one point 54 percent of all the pizzas delivered in the United States. By the mideighties, Domino's was the seventh-largest restaurant chain in the world, the largest privately owned restaurant chain, and the fastest-growing chain. On a personal level, Tom had received just about every award available in the restaurant and franchise industries, and had been awarded a dozen honorary doctorates from sundry universities and colleges. He was selected as the entrepreneur of the decade by the Financial News Television Network, was asked to be on many corporate boards, and gave countless media interviews. According to all worldly criteria, things could hardly get much better. Like the proverbial domino effect, it seemed that one personal triumph led, as if by predestined necessity, to another and another. And yet, as Tom would later confess, the success came at a considerable price. "I started to relax a little too much financially. I realized I could afford virtually anything I wanted, and I got carried away."

The tendency to "splurge" would now reach new levels of self-indulgent excess. Over the next few years, he would spend on a scale of which others could only dream. In 1985, the first phase of Domino's Farms had been completed with a price tag of thirty-six million dollars. Built as Domino's corporate headquarters, it was a monumental office park, spanning 225,000 square feet. By 1997 it would grow to 715,000 square feet and eventually reach its present size of almost 1 million square feet in 2005. In addition to housing Domino's corporate headquarters, it currently has more than fifty other tenants. In keeping with Tom's architectural passion, it had been built in the prairie style of Frank Lloyd Wright and boasts the largest copper roof in the world. It is also the world's longest linear office building, being almost a kilometer (six-tenths of a mile) from one end to the other. He bought a large chunk of Drummond Island in Northern Lake Huron and built a luxurious lodge and golf course on it. He assembled a huge collection of 244 classic cars, including a Bugatti Royale for which he paid over eight million dollars, and the largest collection of Frank Lloyd Wright furniture and artifacts anywhere in the world. As if this were not enough, he also bought a fleet of planes and helicopters and several yachts.

One of Tom's yachts was the venue for a Monaghan family reunion in June 1985 at which forty-two relatives and close family friends were present. The reunion began as a gathering in Tom's private box at Tiger Stadium to see a game, after which the group went aboard the yacht *Tigress* and sailed down the Detroit River to have dinner at Grosse Isle. Tom's mother was present, as was his brother, along with an array of uncles, aunts and cousins. During the reminiscing that tends to dominate such gatherings, Tom's uncle Dan reminded him of the time, as a boy, that Tom had worked all hours to save twenty-five dollars so that he could buy a MacGregor baseball glove. "I was so proud of that glove," Tom remembered, "that for a long time, I used it as a pillow." His Uncle Dan joked that he could have bought a Wilson glove that was less expensive and just as good, perhaps even better. "I admitted that was true," Tom conceded, "but I had wanted to buy the one that cost the most."

"Well," his Uncle Dan said, chuckling as he glanced around at the polished wood and gleaming brass of *Tigress*. "You haven't changed a bit, Tom."

Although one might be reminded in this telling exchange between Tom and his uncle of Oscar Wilde's quip, placed on the lips of Lord Darlington in *Lady Windermere's Fan*, that a cynic is "a man who knows the price of everything and the value of nothing," there is not the slightest strain of cynicism in Tom Monaghan's character. His desire for the most expensive things had more to do with a naïve wish to be recognized as a success in the eyes of the world than in any cynical and clinical measurement of a thing's market price. Indeed, Tom would often pay much more than the market price of something in order to own it, a clear case of putting a thing's value before its price, the very opposite of the motives of the cynic and an indication perhaps of a more than reckless romantic tendency in the ordering of his desires.

Nonetheless, there is a real sense in which the enormous wealth he had accrued as owner of Domino's was causing him to lose touch with more important things, a sense in which the Domino's effect was perhaps a mixed blessing or, perhaps, not a blessing at all. This conundrum or contradiction was evident in an interview Tom gave to *The Detroit Free Press*, published on June 9, 1985, the same month in which he had brandished his opulence at the family reunion on his yacht. "I've always wanted the best," Tom told the reporter who was interviewing him, adding that such a desire was "nothing to brag about." Becoming pensive, he then sought, somewhat inarticulately, to get to grips with the conflict between splurge-spending and holy poverty. "It sounds like a contradiction, and maybe it is with my religious beliefs, but I hope that I haven't—and I'm walking a tightrope here—I hope it's all things I can do without. It's just an enjoyment." It's as though Tom was trying to convince himself, more perhaps than he was trying to convince the reporter, that he could do without the cars, planes, yachts, and other luxuries that he was purchasing and with which he was surrounding himself. His spending on such things was a harmless habit, "an enjoyment." He was not an addict. He was not possessed by his possessions. The fact that Tom was struggling at this point with deep-rooted questions is evident in the manner in which the moment was reported by the interviewer:

> He stops, having awkwardly articulated his personal financial ethics. Then, looking into his lap, he proceeds as softly as if he's talking to God: "I've heard all my life the one saying that it's harder for a rich man to get to heaven than to put a camel through the eye of a needle. I never liked that one.
>
> "But the nuns, when you asked them about it, always said that means you ought to be poor in *spirit*. You ought to be humble. You don't want to worship money or wealth. You just want to do good things with it. No bad things. . . .

"Maybe I don't do all the things I should with my money, that I could, but I hope I don't do any bad things."

The interviewer, seeming intent on exposing his subject as a hypocrite, went on to list all the money Tom was spending on what could be seen as his own self-aggrandizement, including the huge construction costs associated with the building of Domino's Farms, Tom's plans to spend $2 million on tripling the size of his own home, and the $100,000 he'd spent to redecorate his own office. Certainly, whether one felt hostile or otherwise to the lifestyle that Tom was embracing in the heady days of seemingly limitless opulence in which he found himself, it was true, as Tom confessed himself, that his lifestyle could be seen to contradict his religious beliefs and that, at best, he was walking a tightrope when he endeavored, as a Christian, to defend the choices he was making with his money. Apart from the line from Scripture about the camel and the eye of the needle, Tom must surely have been troubled by the teaching of Christ in St. Matthew's Gospel about the temptation to serve Mammon instead of God: "Lay not up to yourselves treasures on earth: where the rust, and moth consume, and where thieves break through and steal. But lay up to yourselves treasures in heaven: where neither the rust nor moth doth consume, and where thieves do not break through, nor steal. For where thy treasure is, there is thy heart also" (Mt 6:19–21), and furthermore, "No man can serve two masters. For either he will hate the one, and love the other: or he will sustain the one, and despise the other. You cannot serve God and mammon" (Mt 6:24).

On April 15, 1985, a few weeks before the interview in *The Detroit Free Press* was published, Tom found himself in Las Vegas, the veritable temple of Mammon, at the Caesars Palace Hotel, as Thomas Hearns prepared for his eagerly awaited showdown with Marvin Hagler, a matchup that was billed as "The War" and is still considered one of the greatest fights of all time. Having been invited into Hearns's locker room in the minutes before the fight, Tom recalled the tension and intensity of the electrified atmosphere as one of the most thrilling moments of his life.

Tom was a keen follower of boxing and had gotten to know Thomas Hearns, known locally in the Detroit area as the "Motor City Cobra" but worldwide as simply "The Hitman," whom he had hosted as his personal guest in his private box at Tigers games. Tom had followed Hearns's meteoric rise, which would make him the first boxer in history to win world titles in four divisions, and was delighted to receive an invitation to be in the locker room in the buildup to the fight. Hearns was surrounded by his handlers while his manager covered him with oil. Tom takes up the story, still excited by the memory thirty years after the event: "It was quite an experience. Quite an experience. His manager was kind of like a painter, paintbrush in hand, and he's painting oil on him, and Tommy is like this; he's just in a trance. And these guys around him are doing this chant. The manager's still putting the oil all over him, and a guy comes up, and all of a sudden, Hearns would say *'Hit me!'* Then he'd go back into a trance. Then he'd say *'Hit me!'*

And I said to the person with me, 'Wow! They certainly know how to prepare psychologically for a fight!' "

Tom then took his seat for what the British fight publication *Boxing News* called "eight minutes of mayhem" and *The Ring* called the "the most electrifying eight minutes ever."

"They say that was the best round in the history of boxing, that first round," Tom says, adding that Hearns broke his hand in the fury of the opening exchanges before eventually being knocked out by Hagler in the third round.

At this time, Tom combined his love of sports with his love of cars when, at the suggestion of Domino's marketing department, he sponsored an Indy race car, which was named the Domino's Pizza Hot One. In 1985, with world-famous driver and two-time Indianapolis 500 winner Al Unser Jr. at the wheel, the Domino's Pizza Team ended the season in second place in the Indy car competition.

In the fall of 1985, Tom took Margie to a car auction in Lancaster, Pennsylvania. He wanted to buy her what he thought was "a cute little '55 Thunderbird," but she was less than impressed, declining the gift. "It's impossible to underestimate my wife's interest in cars," Tom says, adding that it's just as well because "for years she had to drive whatever junk heap of a delivery car I happened to park in our driveway." In truth, as Tom confesses, Margie remained quite happy to drive "junk heaps," running her cars into the ground before replacing them. And yet, in spite of her own lack of interest, and in spite of Tom "talking about cars until it gave Margie a doozy of a headache," she was, Tom wrote, "a good sport about my sudden enthusiasm for buying classic cars," indulging this latest enthusiasm as she had indulged so many other enthusiasms in the past.

In this comparison between Tom and Margie and their respective approach to the trinkets and trappings of wealth, one is tempted to see the two rings that Tom wore, side by side, his twelve-dollar wedding band and his fifty-three-million-dollar World Series ring, as symbolic of the understated simplicity of Margie and the overstated extravagance of Tom. It's as though the two rings signified the defining characteristics of the two spouses. Tom certainly saw the symbolism inherent in the two rings in terms that suggest two sides of his own character. "In many ways, that contrast is symbolic of me and my life. The wedding band reflects the simple and enduring values that are my greatest strength. The World Series ring represents my flamboyant side, the part of me that thrills to bidding against a lot of high rollers for a classic car. My flamboyance isn't an ego trip, it's showmanship."

Tom wrote these words in *Pizza Tiger*, an autobiography published in 1986, which he would later describe as being itself "somewhat of an ego trip." It seems, therefore, that the older Tom Monaghan, looking back across the chasm of the years, would have begged to differ with his younger "flamboyant" self about whether his "splurge spending" was nothing but harmless flamboyance and not an ego trip. He would, however, have agreed with his former self that the simplicity of the wedding band, representing the simplicity of his wife and their married life together, "reflects the simple and enduring values that are my greatest strength." Margie, taken together with Tom's lifelong Catholic faith, was always his greatest strength. The Domino's effect, in contrast, would sometimes betray his greatest weakness.

CHAPTER 11

PIZZA WARS

I N DECEMBER 1985, Tom celebrated twenty-five years as a pizza entrepreneur. Since opening his first store, on December 9, 1960, Domino's had risen to global prominence so that, a quarter of a century later, there were 2,600 stores, spreading across all fifty states and six foreign countries. The company had revenues of $1.4 billion in 1985, and Tom's personal fortune was estimated at around $250 million. It was scarcely surprising that his competitors were eyeing the success of Domino's with increasing interest.

The first shots in what became known as the pizza wars were fired by Arthur G. Gunther, chairman of Pizza Hut, when he told *USA Today* on October 8, 1985, that his company planned to open 1,300 new stores in 1986. Of these new stores, Gunther announced that most would not be conventional restaurants but delivery-only units, designed to compete directly with Domino's dominance in the pizza-delivery business. On the following morning, at a meeting of the Domino's board of franchisees in Las Vegas, Tom held the newspaper aloft, emphasizing Gunther's reference in the article to Domino's as being the "major threat" to Pizza Hut. "We wanted to be in the spotlight," Tom told his senior franchisees, "and now that we *are* in the spotlight, we are a big target. Everybody is taking shots at us." His tone was one of exhilarated defiance, seeing Gunther's declaration of war as a call to action on the part of Domino's. It was time to take the fight to Pizza Hut and to the other corporate pretenders to the pizza-delivery crown.

In *Pizza Tiger*, Tom wrote of Domino's response to Pizza Hut's corporate assault on its market, stating that "we welcome pizza wars": "Competition makes us sharper, keeps us looking for new answers, and prevents us from getting complacent and thinking we know it all. Of course, our twenty-five years of experience in pizza delivery has taught us what most of the problems are. So maybe we make delivery look easy. Maybe we've given some of our competitors the idea that it *is* easy. If so, they're in for a heck of a shock."

It certainly seemed that Domino's had responded vigorously to the new competition from Pizza Hut. All the signs, at least initially, were that growth was continuing to accelerate. By the end of September 1986, Tom was predicting that Domino's would have 3,600 stores by the end of the year, one thousand more than at the same time the previous year, with sales of $2 billion.

The seemingly inexorable rise in Domino's fortunes led to increasing speculation with regard to Tom's own personal fortune. Such speculation, coupled with sensationalist stories of his splurging on anything from cars and airplanes to Frank Lloyd Wright buildings and baseball teams, led to criticism that he was not using his huge wealth for charitable purposes. "I've been criticized from time to time for not being more philanthropic," Tom wrote in 1986. "But the truth is that I take the subject of philanthropy far too seriously to give money away in a scattershot or superficial manner. I want my contributions to be made in the most meaningful way possible." If the right cause presented itself, he was certainly willing to give generously. One such cause was a beleaguered Catholic mission in poverty-stricken Honduras run by a charismatic priest, Fr. Enrique Silvestre.

In 1985, at Fr. Enrique's urging, Tom made the first of a series of trips to Honduras. Arriving in Domino's corporate jet, he was shocked by what he saw: "That first visit gave me a vivid impression of what the dry statistics I'd read about extreme poverty in Honduras mean in terms of human misery. The sight of such widespread need in a country so beautiful and so rich in natural resources is heartrending. I made up my mind that I would do something to help Fr. Enrique change the situation."

Seeing that Fr. Enrique rode from village to village in the mountainous terrain on a malnourished mule, Tom bought him a four-wheel-drive pickup truck, enabling him to visit all the villages in his parish in a single day, compared to the three days that it had taken previously. The truck could also be used by Fr. Enrique to haul supplies and to provide emergency transportation for the isolated villagers. During this first trip, Tom also gave the priest enough money to buy a generator to provide electricity for the remote village of San Juan de los Andes.

Returning in February 1986, Tom was accompanied by two friends, a medical doctor and a dentist, who surveyed the medical and dental needs in Fr. Enrique's parish. Witnessing the faith of the children of the parish at a Mass in the makeshift church, Tom was overwhelmed by the experience. "I wasn't quite prepared for the emotional impact the service would have on me." What made it so powerfully affecting for him were "the ragged children who filled the rough-hewn benches that served as pews. . . . I hadn't felt that kind of spiritual identification with a group of youngsters since I left the orphanage." One can imagine the impact as Tom, who now possessed wealth beyond the wildest imaginings of these impoverished children, recalled his own days of poverty and rejection as a child. In the face of such recognition of a common humanity and a common heritage, the sense of union and communion must have made the trappings of wealth seem superficial in comparison.

Back in the United States, thousands of miles geographically and millions of dollars materially from the impoverished children of Honduras, Tom continued to live the life of a flamboyant millionaire. On January 24, 1986, *The Detroit Free Press* featured an interview with him about his love for the architecture of Frank Lloyd Wright, his having recently purchased two houses that Wright had designed, and on March 4 of that year, a photograph appeared on the front cover of *The Detroit News* of him playing catch with his daughter Susie at the Tigers' spring training camp in Lakeland, Florida. In the following year, on February 3, he was photographed laughing hysterically as world-renowned mime, Marcel Marceau, performed an impromptu skit using pizza dough as his only prop. Marceau was visiting Domino's Farms, the company's recently opened headquarters, to unveil plans that he'd drawn up with Tom for a proposed Marcel Marceau World Center for Mime, which was to be built on the three hundred acres of property surrounding Domino's Farms. A few days later, Tom was criticized by *The Detroit News* in its February 12 issue for donating money to buy computers for the Vatican instead of spending his money on local causes that the paper's columnist deemed more worthy.

In April 1987, Tom turned journalist himself, penning a short article for *Michigan Living* about Drummond Island, one of the largest islands on Lake Huron, a large chunk of which he'd recently purchased as "a place for Domino's team members to meet and generate new ideas." Although Tom had never visited the island prior to the fall of 1985, it had been romantically enshrined in his imagination since childhood because of the stories his uncle Ed had told him of his hunting adventures there before World War II. In spite of such high billing in his imagination, Drummond Island did not disappoint. "I still remember the day I saw the island for the first time. . . . I pulled into the dock, walked up the stairs, and the sights and the sounds were fantastic. I knew right away that I was hooked and that Drummond Island was for me." Having purchased a large property on the island, which became known as Domino's Lodge, on hundreds of acres of wooded land, Tom used his prerogative as landowner to name a three-acre trout pond Lake Marge, after his beloved wife. In the following years, the Lodge became a favorite place for the family to visit during the Christmas holiday season and for a week or so in the summer, as well as for the occasional weekend.

The upbeat nature of the article in *Michigan Living* belied the sobering fact that Domino's was taking a battering in the pizza wars. Contrary to Tom's optimistic predictions, Domino's net income had plummeted to $7.1 million in 1986 from the $15 million earned in the previous year, a dramatic drop in net income of 52 percent. In spite of the downturn in his company's performance, Tom's personal fortune was still considerable. At the beginning of 1988, as estimated by *Forbes*, he was worth $400 million.

A welcome respite from the stress of the pizza wars was provided in the spring of 1987 when Tom had the opportunity to meet the Pope and future saint John Paul II. Tom was in Rome to give a talk at a meeting of the Young Presidents' Organization, an international association of business executives, and while there, at the instigation of Detroit's archbishop, Edmund Szoka, he was invited to a private audience with the Pope. The audience was scheduled to begin with Mass in the Pope's private chapel, and Tom recalled having to rise very early in the morning to get to the Vatican on time. He and his companions were then escorted up various flights of stairs, down corridors and through ornate halls, eventually arriving at what Tom remembered as a "beautiful little gem of a chapel." When they arrived, the Pope was by the altar in private prayer.

Having finished his private devotions, the Holy Father was vested and then celebrated Mass for the twenty or thirty people present. "The really memorable thing was when he gave me Communion," Tom remembers. "His face was right there with mine. He looked into my eyes. He had the Host in his hand to put it on my tongue, and I'll never forget those blue eyes meeting my eyes, this man who was sort of my biggest hero in the world and had been for years."

Tom confessed that his admiration for St. John Paul II was bound up emotionally with the fact that he had been raised by Polish nuns and by his belief that a Polish pope could be instrumental in the restoration of political freedom to the people of Poland and other countries in communist Eastern Europe. He had a feeling that this charismatic pope might be key to the Iron Curtain coming down.

Edified and elated by his meeting with the pope, Tom was inspired on the return flight from Rome to Detroit with the idea of founding an organization of Catholic businessmen. He mentioned this to Fr. Michael Scanlan, president of Franciscan University of Steubenville, Ohio, who came up with the name "Legatus" (the Latin word for "ambassador") for the new organization. In order to be eligible to join Legatus, prospective members needed to be faithful Catholics who were either the president or CEO of a business with at least fifty full-time employees. Dues were $2,500 a year. Eleven people joined in the first year, and Legatus has been growing steadily ever since.

Having met the Pope for the first time in Rome, Tom would meet him again a few months later, in September, during the papal visit to the United States. On this occasion, the venue for the audience was Archbishop Szoka's living room in Detroit, at which Tom handed the Holy

Father a signed copy of his autobiography, *Pizza Tiger*. A
year later, in June 1988, when Archbishop Szoka was in
Rome to be elevated by the Pope to the rank of cardinal,
Tom was unable to attend. He had a previous engagement at
a Domino's regional awards banquet for Domino's employees in Nashville, which he felt duty-bound to attend.

Unable to attend the papal festivities in Rome, Tom
must have been consoled and delighted in May 1988 when
Domino's Pizza was mentioned by another of his heroes,
US President Ronald Reagan. Speaking at the annual
White House News Photographers Association dinner,
the President showed a series of photographs projected on
three huge screens. To the delight of his audience, Reagan
played the stand-up comic, offering captions to the photographs in his role as "the ultimate insider." One picture
showed Reagan standing alongside Soviet leader Mikhail
Gorbachev and pointing to his wristwatch: "You have to
understand, Mikhail, if Domino's doesn't get the pizza here
in thirty minutes, we get it free." As the audience laughed
at Reagan's tongue-in-cheek caption to the photograph,
one could imagine Tom laughing all the way to the bank,
relishing the free publicity. On a more sober note, with
the pizza wars raging, he might also have felt that he and
Domino's could do with all the help they could get.

Publicity of a very different kind was provoked later
the same year when Tom's pro-life views brought him into
open conflict with the radical feminists of the National
Organization for Women. The seeds of conflict were sown
when Tom made a short speech on television in support of
a Michigan ballot proposal to ban state-funded abortions.

Putting his money where his mouth was, he also donated fifty thousand dollars to the campaign. After Michigan voters approved the proposal, the local chapter of the National Organization for Women reacted with fury. Selecting Tom as a scapegoat for their outrage at the pro-life victory in the ballot, NOW organized a nationwide boycott of Domino's stores. Finding himself in hot water politically, Tom had no intention of throwing the proverbial baby out with the bathwater, however hot it became. Willing to sacrifice profits, if necessary, rather than abandon the unborn to the butcher's knife, he held his ground and came out fighting. "One of the best feelings I ever had in my life was when I got news of the national boycott by NOW," he told *The Ann Arbor Observer.** "The first feeling was a fear, a rage—like I was really being attacked where I was hurting. I mean, this is a national boycott against this company that I've been trying to build for so long. But then—this thing happened so fast—it turned into an incredible feeling of peace and joy. Better than I've ever felt in my life. It made me realize why martyrs die with smiles on their faces" (128).

Although Tom was willing to stand by his principles, it is not surprising that many of his franchisees did not want their own profits compromised by his outspoken religious and political views. He received calls, especially from franchisees of those stores serving college campuses where the NOW boycott was most active, attacking him

---

* Quoted in Leonard, *Living the Faith: A Life of Tom Monaghan* (Ann Arbor: University of Michigan Press, 2012). Leonard fails to cite the date of his source.

for undermining their ability to compete in an increasingly competitive market. Already under fire in the pizza wars, Domino's franchisees did not need further blows raining down on them from proabortionists. It seemed, said Tom, that "all the proabortionists in the country were boycotting us, and every liberal, pornographic organization and publication was bombarding us, and many editorials were written about us." And yet, in spite of this, Tom was surprised to discover that more people supported his pro-life stand than condemned it:

> We used to get a lot of mail, more than we could ever tally, tens of thousands of letters. One day, we decided to take a large chunk of it and tally it. We found that it was something like sixteen to one in *our* favor! This was despite the fact that much of the opposition mail was organized. In one case we got a whole box of letters, each one the same except for the signature. We counted every one of them. The positive ones seemed to all be spontaneous and individual. Still the big margin was in our favor.

Regardless of whether the NOW boycott had been effective in harming Domino's as a means of punishing Tom for his dissident views on abortion, there was little doubt that the company was suffering the harmful effects of the pizza wars. Tom confessed that sales were "anemic" at the time and that "we were going through a tough time." In an interview with James Leonard, Don Vlcek, a long-serving senior executive with Domino's, was even more candid in his description of the state of the company at the end of the 1980s: "The company had lost its magic. It almost seemed like before that everything Tom touched turned to gold. But now, things went from turning to gold to turning to . . . well, let's just say that Domino's started to falter. Pizza Hut and Little Caesars were expanding, and the franchisees were getting hit" (8).

For many of those involved with Domino's, it appeared that the golden years of the previous decade belonged to a golden age that was passing away. For many of the franchisees, embattled and embittered, it seemed that the pizza wars were being lost.

CHAPTER 12

DEATH AND RESURRECTION

A S THE pizza wars raged in the foreground of Tom's life, his mother's ailing health cast a deathly shadow in the background, exposing the emotional scars of his troubled childhood.

Throughout 1988, Anna Monaghan's health deteriorated. "She knew she was dying," Tom remembers. "She had cancer. It was going through her whole body. She was very calm about it and apparently felt ready to be with the Lord." Wishing to get her spiritual house in order before she died, she showed Tom the things among her personal possessions that she wanted him and his brother, Jim, to have, expressing a strong desire that her two sons work harder to get along. Taking his mother's words to heart, Tom contacted Jim, from whom he'd become somewhat estranged, and arranged for them to meet at her bedside. At Tom's instigation, the two sons said the Rosary at their dying mother's side. "She couldn't talk, but she could understand. I felt very good that she could hear the two of us saying the Rosary."

Having witnessed the reconciliation of her two sons at her bedside, praying for her soul as she approached the end of her mortal life, Anna Monaghan died shortly afterward, no doubt happier and more at peace for having witnessed in extremis the family unity that heretofore had been so sadly lacking. She was seventy-three years old.

A few days after his mother's death, an article appeared in *The Ann Arbor News* highlighting Tom's "estranged relationship" with her. Tom thought it "very unfair" and phoned the newspaper to complain about it. Acknowledging the difficulties of his childhood, during which it could indeed be said that they had an "estranged relationship," he protested that, as an adult, he was "always respectful and cordial." They might not have been very close, seeing each other rarely even though they lived in the same town, but they always got together over the Christmas holidays. "We'd invite her over for the holidays," said Tom. "She'd have us over on Christmas Eve." And yet, in spite of Tom's protests, he confessed to his cousin Diane Mahler that the hardest thing he ever did was tell his mother that he loved her. Asked about this by his biographer James Leonard, Tom could not recall that he had ever told his mother that he loved her, but had he ever done so, it was probably when she was on her deathbed: "I'm not saying I didn't say it. I can see why it wouldn't be really easy to do. My relationship with my mother was. . . ." His voice trailed off, trying to find the right thoughts and the right way to put them into words. "I think one of my big regrets in my life was that I didn't have more respect for my mother at the time" (363). By "at the time," he was referring to his childhood. When I asked him about his relationship with his mother and whether he had any guilt or lingering resentment, he reiterated the same sense of regret that he'd expressed to Leonard: "I'm always embarrassed about the way I treated her when I was younger. When she had her temper tantrums and started yelling at me, I didn't just sit there; you know, I'd holler back at her."

Whether or not one believes that Tom could be seen as truly culpable, considering his mother's neglect of him and her acts of verbal violence, it says much for the gentleness of his Christian spirit that he blames himself and not her. Indeed, he goes to great lengths to defend his mother whenever he senses that she's being maligned. Take, for instance, his response when asked how he was able to love a mother who kept rejecting him. "I wouldn't call it rejecting me," he replied, explaining that his mother suffered from depression, or what would now be called bipolar disorder. "Just highs and lows. I mean, she could be very enthusiastic, an incurable romantic, or she could go into a temper tantrum, grab a broom, and start chasing me. . . . All my life people have been criticizing my mother for the way I was treated when I was a boy. I don't think that's fair. She was a good woman. She always meant well. She just had these tantrums, her funny ways. That's all." Once again, he turned the finger of blame upon himself: "I'm ashamed to say that, particularly in my teenage years, I was embarrassed to be around her. She didn't know how to dress. She didn't have social skills. She seemed to be in her own world. But she was a good woman."

But was it hard to love her?

"I don't know about the definition of *love* in this case. I would say I loved her. I remember when she was dying someone told me that I should take that opportunity, and it could've been then when I said I loved her. I remember I spent some time with her there [at her bedside]. I felt that was something I really should do. I believe I had some things that I should say that maybe weren't easy for me, you know, maybe say 'I love you.'"

In drawing the curtain on Tom's relationship with his mother, which of course can never really be done while Tom retains any memories of her, it might be worth revisiting Tom's questioning of the definition of "love." On the one hand, love can be seen as a *feeling*, as something essentially *irrational*; on the other hand, in the Christian sense, love can be seen as an *action*, as an essentially *rational choice*, something that is *done* and not *felt*. In the irrational sense of the word, Tom retained all sorts of conflicting feelings about his mother and his relationship with her. There were regrets and the guilt that goes with them, and perhaps recriminations and the remnant of resentment that accompanies them. Such feelings are the consequence of the mixed-up meltdown that takes place when the maternal–filial bond is broken or loosened by sin, the mess that selfishness causes. In the rational sense of the word, the Christian understanding of love as a freely chosen, self-sacrificial action, Tom's defense of his mother's reputation and his telling her that he loved her are acts of true love in spite of whatever irrational feelings accompanied them. Indeed, the harder it was for Tom to tell his mother that he loved her, the greater was the act of love when he did so.

As is so often the case, the close encounter with death and the questions it raises can lead to a spiritual resurrection.

In Tom's case, this resurrection came about in 1989 with his reading of *Mere Christianity* by C. S. Lewis and the life-changing impact that it was to have on him. Lewis's work of popular Christian apologetics was not the sort of book that Tom would usually have read. In the past, he'd spent most of his time reading self-help books or biographies of successful businessmen, such as the autobiography of Ray Kroc, which he'd asked Kroc to sign when they'd met in San Diego, or, in a similar vein, *Quest for the Best* by Stanley Marcus, president of the luxury retailer Neiman Marcus, which Tom had "really enjoyed" when it was published in 1979. "I can't believe how much I got into having the best of everything," Tom says. "I must have become one of the most knowledgeable people about what was best. I enjoyed *The Robb Report* and such magazines. I had to know where the best hotels and restaurants were everywhere I traveled. I loved shopping around the world." Looking back on this epicurean obsession from the perspective of a more temperate maturity, he confesses that he is "not proud of such interests," realizing that he'd allowed them to consume too much of his time and passion.

The initial desire to expand his intellectual and spiritual horizons through the reading of appropriate books was prompted by his friendship with a young Catholic intellectual, Dinesh D'Souza, whom Tom had appointed to the board of the newly established Domino's Foundation (which would later be renamed the Ave Maria Foundation). In 1986, D'Souza had published a slim volume, entitled *The Catholic Classics*, designed as an introduction to ten of the most important Catholic works ever published. These were Augustine's *Confessions*, Boethius's *Consolation of Philosophy*, Bede's *Ecclesiastical History of the English People*, Aquinas's *Summa Theologica*, Dante's *Divine Comedy*, Pascal's *Pensées*, Thomas à Kempis's *Imitation of Christ*, Newman's *Apologia Pro Vita Sua*, Chesterton's *Orthodoxy*, and Merton's *Seven Storey Mountain*. Tom made a noble effort to acquaint himself with each of these ten books, though one wonders how far he got into the works of Augustine or Aquinas, or how long he struggled with Bede's Anglo-Saxon history or Boethius's conversations with the Lady Philosophy or Dante's descent and ascent into the depths and heights of scholasticism. Certainly, on looking back on his efforts to immerse himself in the Catholic intellectual tradition, it is perhaps significant and hardly surprising that the two works that he chooses to single out for particular mention from this list are those by G. K. Chesterton and Thomas Merton, which are not only the most modern, being the only titles in D'Souza's list that were published in the twentieth century, but indubitably the most accessible to the modern reader. It would, however, be a book that was not on D'Souza's list that would have by far the biggest life-changing impact.

Although Lewis's *Mere Christianity* could not be listed specifically as a *Catholic* classic, its author being an Anglican, few would venture to suggest that it does not deserve a place on any list of Christian classics. Tom had read it at D'Souza's suggestion and was particularly moved by the chapter of the book dealing with the sin of pride, which Lewis called "The Great Sin." Tom had always been taught that pride "was the greatest of all sins and the source of all sins" but what was earth-shattering was the way in which Lewis illustrated that much of Tom's own motivation to succeed was rooted in this very sin, which was the worst and the deadliest sin of all. As Tom read Lewis's words of wisdom, it was as if they were being addressed to him personally, as if Lewis had become his own personal spiritual adviser:

> C. S. Lewis said that the reason I wanted the luxuries wasn't for their convenience or their beauty but solely because I wanted to impress people. I seemed to have two phases: first to go to the point that I wasn't embarrassed and just blend in, but in the next millisecond I was dissatisfied with that state and wanted to stand out above the others. I hated to show off and would go out of my way to not look like a show-off, but in reality I was the biggest show-off of all. In fact, over the years, this was my most confessed sin in the confessional: trying to impress people. C. S. Lewis put me in my place.

Considering how important the short chapter on pride in *Mere Christianity* is to Tom's life, it would behoove us well to look at it in more detail, imagining its impact on Tom as we do so. Lewis begins thus: "There is one vice of which no man in the world is free; which every one in the world loathes when he sees it in someone else; and of which hardly any people, except Christians, ever imagine they are guilty of themselves. . . . There is no fault which makes a man more unpopular, and no fault which we are more unconscious of in ourselves. And the more we have it ourselves, the more we dislike it in others."

Having shown us an image of our darkened selves, with the great mastery of human psychology that he would show in works such as *The Screwtape Letters*, Lewis hits us with the realization that this narcissism, which we ignore at our peril, is the worst sin of all and the mark of the devil in us: "According to Christian teachers, the essential vice, the utmost evil, is Pride. Unchastity, anger, greed, drunkenness, and all that, are mere fleabites in comparison: it was through Pride that the devil became the devil: Pride leads to every other vice: it is the complete anti-God state of mind."

Then, as if Lewis had Tom in mind as he wrote, he hits the proverbial nail on the head: "The point is that each person's pride is in competition with every one else's pride. It is because I wanted to be the big noise at the party that I am so annoyed at someone else being the big noise. . . . Now what you want to get clear is that Pride is *essentially* competitive—is competitive by its very nature. . . . Pride gets no pleasure out of having something, only out of having more of it than the next man." The words struck home, retaining their impact, as is clear as we repeat Tom's recollection of their power more than twenty years later: *C. S. Lewis said that the reason I wanted the luxuries wasn't for their convenience or their beauty but solely because I wanted to impress people. . . . I hated to show off and would go out of my way to not look like a show off, but in reality I was the biggest show off of all.*

To cease to be proud, to attain humility, is not only a gift but a liberation. As Lewis put it, it is "feeling the infinite relief of having for once got rid of all the silly nonsense about your own dignity which has made you restless and unhappy all your life." It was necessary, Lewis insisted, by the grace of God, "to take off a lot of silly, ugly, fancy-dress in which we have all got ourselves up and are strutting about like the little idiots we are." Pointing the finger at himself, Lewis confessed that he was as much in need of this as the next man: "I wish I had got a bit further with humility myself: if I had, I could probably tell you more about the relief, the comfort, of taking the fancy-dress off—getting rid of the false self, with all its 'Look at me' and 'Aren't I a good boy?' and all its posing and posturing."

Reading these words as a middle-aged man who, in the eyes of the world, was hugely successful, Tom was cut to the quick, stunned with a sense of mortification: "I thought I was a pretty good guy. I worked hard, I didn't have the normal bad habits, didn't drink or smoke, and didn't chase women. I practiced my faith, at least the minimum: Mass every Sunday and Holy Day, the required numbers of confessions per year." In fact, and self-deprecation aside, he had long since exceeded the minimum requirements with regard to the practice of the Faith. He had been going to daily Mass for years, he said three Rosaries every day, and he didn't eat meat on Fridays, abstaining year-round, not merely during Lent. The point was, as C. S. Lewis had shown him, that these pious practices, good as they were, were not good enough. More was needed. Unto those to whom much is given, much is expected. "My number one goal in life was to become a good Catholic. Well, I finally hit a home run with *Mere Christianity* and got to the heart of one of the main things I needed spiritually: facing up to the sin of pride and doing something about it."

Having read Lewis's book, he saw his life and the way he was living it from a new perspective. He realized that he couldn't have it both ways. He couldn't offer himself to Christ and His Church and at the same time remain so attached to the luxurious trappings of wealth. "I was walking a tightrope during the eighties, trying to enjoy everything this life offered and trying to be a good Catholic. I realized at one point what I wanted to be was a billionaire saint. I figured I could get along without the luxuries, that I wasn't addicted to them." Like an alcoholic or a compulsive gambler who is finally forced to confront the lie that he'd been living, Lewis had shown that he was addicted, or at least unhealthily attached, to the luxuries that money could buy. Now he realized that the tightrope he was walking could easily become the rope with which he hung himself.

> I look back on that part of my life and realize how foolish I was. I'm ashamed of it. What happened to me? I always thought when success came that I was one guy who would be able to handle it. After all, I had my five priorities, I worked on my faith, I didn't mistreat people, I always made an attempt to be nice to people, not lose my temper, I read a lot, I exercised and took care of my health, I always knew these things were more important than my pocketbook.

> I look back now and see how I floundered after I
> became successful.

It was time to make a choice between the good life and the life of luxury; the life of virtue, which is inseparable from the cross of suffering, or the life of comfort, which can easily become the path of least resistance that leads to hell. To his credit, Tom chose the better part and made what he calls his "millionaire's vow of poverty." "I decided to give up all ostentatious luxuries, not conveniences, but 'show off' luxuries. No more interest in driving Ferraris and Rolls-Royces—no more flying first-class."

Regarding the last of these luxuries that Tom forsook following what might be called his "born-again" experience after reading C. S. Lewis, the present author can personally testify to Tom's continued spurning of first-class travel more than fifteen years after this initial resolution was made. I was at the departure gate for a flight from Detroit to Fort Myers, Florida, when Tom approached me. He and I were on the same flight. We chatted affably until it was time to board. I had been upgraded to first class, a perk that goes with flying frequently, and was surprised that Tom was not also flying first-class. He told me that he never flew first-class and that he always booked the middle seat in the main cabin because it afforded additional opportunities to evangelize his fellow passengers. Although he didn't say so, it was clear to me that he also chose the middle seat as an additional mortification. Having heard many negative stories about Tom from those who felt, justly or unjustly, that he'd treated them badly, I was greatly edified to see this practical example of his holiness, or at least his working hard to attain it. For my part, the miserable sinner that I am, I still rejoice whenever I'm upgraded to first class and always try to sit in the aisle seat, avoiding the middle seat like the proverbial plague! Needless to say, to the eyes of the world, moving from a private jet or the driver's seat in a Ferrari to the middle seat in the main cabin of today's cramped airplanes is a sign of how the mighty have fallen. For the Christian, rejoicing in the exaltation of the humble, it is a sign of the fallen becoming mighty in the eyes of God, through His grace working in the lives of those who love Him.

As this one personal anecdote illustrates, Tom's reading of Lewis's *Mere Christianity* was literally life changing. In following Lewis's advice "to take off a lot of silly, ugly, fancy-dress in which we have all got ourselves up" and in ceasing all the "strutting about like the little idiots we are," Tom was making the necessary Christian choice to die to the things of this world that we might live for the things of the world to come. He was choosing death to self so that he might enjoy the resurrection that comes with self-denial. He was following in the literary example of King Lear, who stripped himself naked with the words "off, off, you lendings," forsaking the borrowed things that we can't take with us when we die for the everlasting things that will take us to heaven, and of course, he was also following the example of St. Francis, who also stripped himself naked, forsaking the wealth of his affluent family so that he could become wedded to Lady Poverty.

Henceforth, Tom would no longer walk the tightrope, trying perilously to balance the luxurious show-off things of this world with the necessary things of God. Instead, he would forsake the tightrope for the straight and narrow path that leads to heaven.

CHAPTER 13

DOMINO SERVIENTE

Sollicitudine non pigri spiritu ferventes Domino
serviente.
*In carefulness not slothful. In spirit fervent. Serving
the Lord.*

Rom 12:11

AS THE present author owes his own conversion, in
part, to the works and wisdom of C. S. Lewis, it is
gratifying to know that he has this much in common with
Tom Monaghan. Indeed, we both have this much in common with numerous other people, from all walks of life,
who owe their conversion or reawakening to Christianity to the influence of Lewis. And although Lewis was an
Anglican, it is astonishing how many converts to Catholicism owe their conversion, at least in part and under grace,
to Lewis's influence. The great American literary convert,
Walker Percy, commenting on the numerous converts who
had come to Catholicism through the writings of C. S.
Lewis, remarks that "writers one might expect, from Aquinas to Merton," are mentioned frequently as influences,

"but guess who turns up most often? C. S. Lewis!—who, if he didn't make it all the way, certainly handed over a goodly crew."

Some of the "goodly crew" to whom Percy alludes, those who have been influenced on their paths to Rome by C. S. Lewis, include E. F. Schumacher, Al Kresta, Fr. Dwight Longenecker, Sheldon Vanauken, Warren Carroll, Thomas Howard, Bobby Jindal, Peter Kreeft, Bernard Nathanson, Gene Wolfe and Walter Hooper, to name but an illustrious few. Tom Monaghan, it must be remembered, is not a convert but a cradle Catholic, yet his encounter with Lewis can certainly be said to have caused a major conversion of heart and mind, reorienting the prideful soul toward Christ and the needs of His Church.

Having made his "millionaire's vow of poverty," Tom's priorities changed radically. At the time of his reading of *Mere Christianity*, he was in the midst of building the home of his dreams. "I was about one-and-a-half years into the construction of our house," he recalls. "It was about one-third complete. I had already spent over seven million dollars—after reading *Mere Christianity*, I stopped construction." The hardest thing was breaking the news to the architect, E. Fay Jones, who had studied under Frank Lloyd Wright and with whom Tom had struck up a good friendship. "It's amazing how this vow changed my life," Tom remembers. "Life became so much simpler. It was probably a lot like stopping drugs. It was a relief. I sold the airplanes, the yachts, the Frank Lloyd Wright collection, and the car collection."

In an interview in the July 1989 issue of *Gentlemen's Quarterly*, he insisted that he was putting his religious beliefs before his business interests because "that's what I care about most." Discussing the ways in which he tried to practice his Christian principles in the context of his business, he spoke about fairness and about treating people well. "In other words, I try not to let power corrupt." Above all, he wanted to be seen as a Catholic first and a businessman second. "The most flattering thing anyone can say about me is that I'm a good Catholic."

Not everyone was happy with this change of direction. On July 2 of that same year, *The Detroit News*, seldom the friendliest of voices, stated that Tom's past reputation for splurging on classic cars and real estate was "almost understandable," comparing his excessive spending with the escapades of the fictional Jay Gatsby, but what was much less forgivable in the view of the newspaper's acidic and acerbic journalist was Tom's funding of pro-life causes. "Last fall, Monaghan donated $50,000 to the Committee to End State-Funded Abortions, which won its recent referendum. When you're eating your next pizza, remember, all the pepperonis go to Tom's pet political projects." Another reason that Tom had earned a place on *The Detroit News'* list of "ten Detroiters we could do without" was his controversial plans to build a new stadium for the Tigers, thereby offending the sentimental sensibilities of Tigers fans who were understandably attached to the old stadium. Riding this wave of discontent, *The Detroit News*, posing as the voice of the people, waxed indignant: "Perhaps the biggest rub of all is what Tom's thinking of doing to Tiger Stadium. The

Tigers are his team, all right, but somehow the ballpark belongs to all of us. Just the thought of the venerable field on Michigan and Trumbull being replaced by a swank, new suburban location—one with a bigger and better box for the owner, we imagine—is enough to make us cry foul."

On October 9, Tom appeared on *Donahue*, the long-running TV talk show, the highlight of which was the delivery of a pizza that host Phil Donahue had ordered live on air, the delivery driver arriving with the pizza only seconds before the deadline of Domino's widely advertised thirty-minute delivery promise. A few weeks before this high-profile appearance on prime-time TV, Tom had shocked the business world by announcing his intention of selling Domino's, having been at the helm for almost thirty years and having seen it grow from a tiny operation in a single pizza store in Ypsilanti, Michigan, to a global corporation with thousands of stores worldwide. "I announced I was selling the company. I was spending more and more time on my foundation. I felt it was time to cash out and spend the rest of my life serving the Church."

Tom was fifty-two at the time and was yearning with his "millionaire's vow of poverty" to answer the call that God had made to St. Francis to "rebuild my church." Selling Domino's would give him the cash he needed to concentrate on his charitable work. "My theory was that I'd have a chunk of cash and the Detroit Tigers. The Tigers were a better door opener than Domino's. I was known more by this time as the owner of the Tigers than I was for being the owner of Domino's. The Tigers were a tiny operation compared to Domino's and thus didn't need the kind of attention a large pizza chain did, so I'd be free to pursue my philanthropic efforts."

Having announced his decision to sell Domino's, Tom waited expectantly for the offers to come in from potential buyers. Nothing happened. Amid the backdrop of the trial of the high-flying financier Michael Robert Milken, who had been indicted by a federal grand jury on ninety-eight counts of racketeering and fraud in March 1989 and would plead guilty to six counts of securities and tax violations in April 1990, the market was relatively moribund. "My timing was terrible," says Tom. "This was the time when Milken went to jail and all leveraged buyouts disappeared. The banks were in the worst trouble since the depression. Insurance companies, usually a major source of financing of large business deals, dried up."

In many respects, the whole scenario became a comedy of errors. It took Tom and his team six months to decide who should handle the sale. Unable to decide whether to hire Morgan Bank or Goldman Sachs, they eventually decided to hire both. "That was a big mistake," Tom recalls. "Neither of them had the maximum incentive nor authority to run with it." With no bigtime buyers showing any interest, the decision was made to sell Domino's to its employees, in what is known as an ESOP, an Employee Stock Option Plan, a scenario that would have dovetailed well with the Church's social teaching on subsidiarity and producers' cooperatives. Unfortunately, Prudential Insurance, who had been selected as the financing source, failed to follow through. "After a long period of time, they backed out, partly because Domino's sales were dropping and partly because of the insurance industry troubles."

As the sale of Domino's stalled, bogged down in a quagmire of delays, Tom found great solace in the various Church-related projects that he was now pursuing with renewed and energized vigor. In 1990, at the request of Bernard Cardinal Law of Boston, he traveled to Nicaragua to meet Miguel Cardinal Obando y Bravo. He agreed to finance the building of a new cathedral in Managua to replace the one that had been effectively destroyed in an earthquake almost twenty years earlier. Construction began in August 1991, and the cathedral was consecrated for worship a little over two years later. The final construction costs were $4.5 million, of which Tom paid $3.5 million. Still in Central America, Tom financed the building of a chapel, a clinic, a pharmacy, a farm, and a ceramics workshop in Honduras. The ceramics workshop produced Catholic religious artifacts for sale in the United States, and the profits from the farm financed the training of new priests.

Back in the United States and at the other end of the financial spectrum, Legatus, the organization for Catholic CEOs that Tom had founded in 1987 with only eleven members and their spouses, was going from strength to strength. Assisted by Tom's foundation's $634,000 contribution in 1989, Legatus had grown to a membership of 225 by 1990. Membership remained restrictive, being open only to presidents or CEOs of businesses with at least thirty employees (this was changed from the earlier threshold of fifty) and an annual revenue of at least $4 million (up from $3 million in 1987). Among its celebrity members were former baseball commissioner Bowie Kuhn and Dallas Cowboys great Roger Staubach. From around this time, Tom took an annual delegation from Legatus to meet Pope John Paul II in Rome, meeting the future saint many times in the following years.

Another beneficiary of Tom's munificence was Mother Angelica, the feisty Franciscan foundress of the Eternal Word Television Network (EWTN), who had gotten into financial difficulties. Responding to her appeal for help, he traveled to the Network's studio in Alabama and agreed to loan her one million dollars. Later, with the financial crisis resolved, the loan was duly and dutifully repaid. It is sobering to contemplate that Tom's timely intervention might have saved EWTN in its infancy from an untimely demise. How many millions of people would have been deprived of the televisual blessings that the Network has provided over the years had he not been there to help?

Although his efforts to sell Domino's were stalling, Tom reiterated his new spiritual priorities in an interview with *The Ann Arbor Observer*, stating that he wanted "to free up my time for the foundation. That's my whole objective. I've completely lost interest in making money for myself. I'm completely cured. I always had in the back of my mind that I was going to use my millions to give away anyhow, and now I'm there."

Freeing up his time from his other more worldly commitments would not be easy. Apart from his ownership of Domino's and the Detroit Tigers, he was still sponsoring the Domino's Pizza Hot One on the Indy car racing circuit. On May 27, 1990, his car, driven by Arie Luyendyk, won the Indianapolis 500, arguably the most prestigious prize in world motorsports. The Hot One not only won but did so by breaking the record for the fastest average speed in the history of the race, 186 miles per hour, a record that would not be broken until 2013. In spite of such success, Tom withdrew sponsorship that very year, ensuring that he bowed out in a blaze of glory.

There was, however, to be no bowing out in a blaze of glory from Domino's, which was floundering badly in his absence. He had hoped to show that the company could prosper without him, but he had only proved that it couldn't, at least not at that time. General and administrative expenses, which had averaged around six or seven million dollars a month on his watch, had ballooned to several times this number by August 1991. Domino's book value had plummeted to only nine million dollars, and the company's long-term debt had risen to seventy-four million dollars. At year's end, Domino's recorded a pretax loss of forty-eight million dollars, comparing catastrophically with the sixty-three million dollars in profits that the company had made between 1980 and 1990, when Tom had been at the helm. Clearly nobody would want to buy the company under these dire circumstances. There was no escape, as he had hoped, from being a pizza baron to becoming a full-time philanthropist. At least not yet. The exit strategy would have to be put on hold, and Tom would need to take back the reins to prevent Domino's from careering into what might have proven a terminal decline. On December 7, 1991, he announced that he would be returning to Domino's full-time.

"My first full year back was a bloodbath," he remembers. "We sold off many losing corporate stores to franchisees to become franchise stores. Those we couldn't sell or give away, we closed." The drastic measures were necessary to avert disaster, and once again, Tom proved himself a master at turning things around. Although the company was smaller, with around 4,500 stores compared to the 5,000 or so when he had taken back the reins, it was much healthier. From May 1993 onward, Domino's was once again recording record profits. During this time, they were in discussions with their banks, and on July 27, 1994, they brought in a new bank group. "We had a big celebration," Tom remembers, "calling it Domino's Deliverance Day and celebrated it each year." Much of the company's debt was paid off, and same store sales increases were the highest of all national restaurant chains. The strong year-over-year same-store sales increased until Tom sold the company in 1998. According to John Gilbertson from Goldman Sachs, Tom had engineered the most dramatic and complete transformation he had seen in all his years in Wall Street.

The remarkable recovery of Domino's fortunes came at considerable personal cost, not least of which was his reluctant decision to sell the Tigers:

> I really messed up. Owning the Tigers was a dream
> come true, but I messed up because that's something
> you want to have in your family a long time, particu-
> larly with someone like my daughter Susie, who was
> working full-time for the Tigers. It was her life. It
> really bothered me that I kind of pulled the rug out

from under her by selling them. I got myself into a situation where I probably had to. The banks were putting a lot of pressure on me. I had a lot of debt, about a half a billion in debt, and it was going to be a little bit of a public bloodbath to work my way out of it. I thought I could get Domino's back on track, but during the process, I was going to have to really streamline everything, and that meant that I wasn't able to give the Tigers the kind of support you want to give them to be able to afford the players they need to compete at the highest level. I definitely didn't want to do so, but I put myself in a situation where I had to sell.

As Tom poured forth his regrets, clearly feeling the pain of letting his daughter down, even after all these years, he seemed to see that this hard and reluctant decision might have been a blessing in disguise. "But, on the other hand," he adds, almost as an afterthought, "owning them was still an ego trip, and I'm better off without the things that would give me adulation. Owning a major sports franchise, it's almost like being pumped with royal blood." He pauses, as if digging deeper into his soul. "Better off without it."

As it became clear that Tom intended to sell the Tigers, there was much speculation regarding who would become the new owner. It was rumored that Edsel Ford II, executive director of the Ford Motor Company and great-grandson of Henry Ford, would purchase the team, but after months of secret negotiations, Tom decided to sell the franchise to Mike Ilitch, founder of the Detroit pizza

chain Little Caesars, one pizza baron selling to another.
Tom received eighty-three million dollars in cash from his
rival and a further twenty million dollars in assumed obli-
gations. Having paid fifty-three million dollars for the club
nine years earlier, he had made a clear profit of more than
fifty million dollars from the sale, in addition to the forty
million dollars in profit he had made over the nine years
he owned the club. The huge profit was a reflection of the
success that the Tigers had enjoyed under Tom's ownership.
During his years in charge, the Tigers' winning percentage was 52 percent, considerably better than the previous
nine years' average of 43.8 percent and much better than
the even lower average of 41.8 percent in the following nine
years under Ilitch's ownership. In spite of the bad press he
had been getting in recent years for his plans to build a new
stadium and the hostility of many fans who were nostalgi-
cally attached to the old one, his time in charge of the club
can be seen as a golden era in its history, a record that Tom
has every right to look back on with immense satisfaction.

The enormous profit from the sale of the Tigers helped
to keep the bankers off his back as he tried to steer Domino's back onto an even keel, and it also helped to offset
the loss he made in the selling of his classic car collection
and in the selling of the three-thousand-acre property on
Drummond Island, which was also off-loaded in the water-
shed year of 1992. Regarding the latter, it was sold for three
million dollars, a mere pittance compared to the thirty million dollars that Tom had invested in it.

Looking back on the three years since his reading of
Mere Christianity and the "millionaire's vow of poverty" it

had inspired, Tom could not have foreseen how many difficulties lay in his path as he sought to fulfill his promise to God that he would use his wealth to help build the
Church. Once again, he had been called to save Domino's,
steering it through yet another of the crises that had beset
it over the years. Having done so, remarkably and, some
might be tempted to say, miraculously, he finally found
himself in a position where he would be able to sell the
company to which he had given birth more than thirty
years earlier. In doing so, and mindful of the pun on the
name of Domino's in the original Latin (Domino meaning
"the Lord"), he could say with St. Paul in the latter's letter
to the Romans that he was "not slothful, was fervent in
spirit, and was serving the Lord."

Tom's parents' wedding day,
1936

Tom and Margie's wedding day,
1962

Seventh-grade photo at Immaculate Conception School in
Traverse City, Michigan. Tom is third from the right in the back row.

Semper Fidelis

Domino's store on Cross Street

An early delivery car

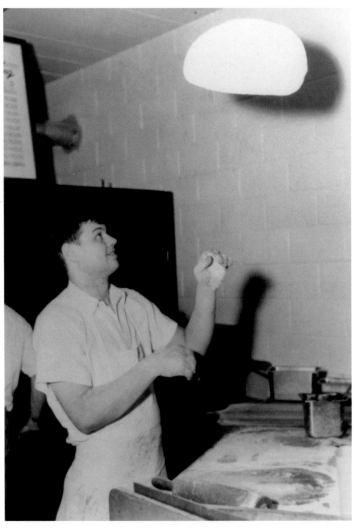

Perfecting pie-tossing technique

Working the oven

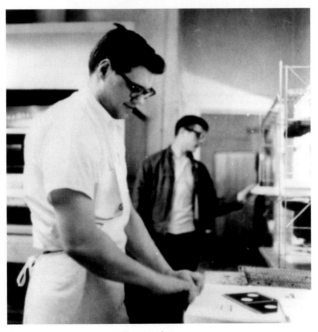

Boxing 'em up

Early advertising effort

Showing off the logo

Celebrating the opening of the three-hundredth store
(under the name Pizza Dispatch because of the Amstar lawsuit)

Managing a growing company

The smile says it all.

Tossing a pie in the late '90s, prior to selling the company

Domino's Farms Office Park in Ann Arbor Township—
from a vision to a reality

Domino's Farms Office Park in Ann Arbor Township—
from a vision to a reality

Opposite and above: Tom celebrating the 1984 World Series with
former Detroit Tigers owner John Fetzer

Tom receiving an award at the Pontifical Catholic University
of Puerto Rico, 1998

Al Kresta interviewing Tom at Ave Maria Radio's studio in Ann Arbor

Reconnecting with Sister Mary Berarda

Tom and youngest daughter, Barbara, with
Sister Mary Berarda in 1983

Breaking ground on the Dominican Sisters of Mary, Mother of the Eucharist's motherhouse in Ann Arbor with Mother Mary Assumpta Long, OP (other sisters behind)

Meeting Mother Teresa of Calcutta

To Tom Monaghan with best wishes *Geo Bush*

Meeting with President George H. W. Bush

Visiting Supreme Court Justice Clarence Thomas
Left to right: Bernard Dobranski, Paul Roney, Justice Thomas, Thomas Monaghan, Nicholas Healy, Richard Thompson, Stephen Beal

Two of Tom's meetings with Pope John Paul II

Greeting Pope Benedict XVI

Meeting Pope Francis for the first time

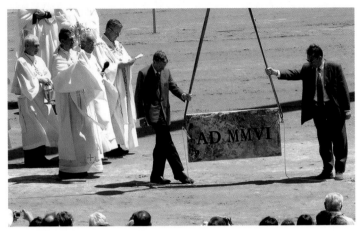

Placing the cornerstone of the Oratory in Ave Maria with Nick Healy

Ribbon-cutting ceremony for Ave Maria University
at its permanent campus, August 2007

Nick and Jane Healy, Bishop Frank Dewane, and Tom
touring the Oratory during its construction

The Oratory's construction, well under way

The Ave Maria Oratory

Bird's-eye view of the Oratory

CHAPTER 14

EDUCATION AS IF TRUTH MATTERED

W ITH DOMINO'S once more cruising along in a sea of profit, Tom was able to concentrate on his various philanthropic interests. He had long been interested in Catholic education, being dismayed at the poor catechesis being offered at Fr. Gabriel Richard High School in Ann Arbor, Michigan, for which he had been a board member since the early 1980s. He also served on the board of several Catholic colleges. "I had been on seven college and university boards over the years," Tom says, "so I was getting a little feel for academia." He was particularly inspired by the transformation of Franciscan University of Steubenville under the leadership of its president, Fr. Michael Scanlan, whom Tom described as "a big hero of mine.": "He took a dying institution, Steubenville College, and converted it into Franciscan University. Cardinal O'Connor called it the preeminent Catholic university in the United States. I agree. He did it despite tremendous obstacles. They had a lot of debt, virtually no endowment, faculty problems and little spiritual activity. In fact, it was rated by *Playboy*

Magazine as one of the top ten party schools in the country. It was on the verge of closing."

The astonishing transformation of Franciscan University throughout the 1980s seemed to offer a model for other Catholic schools to emulate. Too many Catholic schools were neglecting their Catholic identity and mission, or "dropping the ball" as Tom put it. "Not only were they not teaching the faith, they were undermining it." He was especially dismayed in discussions with his good friend, Ralph Martin, to learn of the damage done by modernist theologians, such as Fr. Richard McBrien, at Notre Dame. Impassioned by a desire to "stop the rot" in Catholic higher education, he decided to use his considerable financial resources as a means of supporting orthodox renewal in academe.

He had been flattered when Cardinal Szoka had asked him to join the board of the Catholic University of America. "After all, this was the bishops' university. About half of the board is made up of cardinals, archbishops, and bishops." Surely, he thought, this university, at least, was in safe hands. He was, however, to be disillusioned very quickly. "They obviously expected me to make significant financial contributions but, compared to Franciscan University, CUA seemed like a secular university at the time. Meeting after meeting, I heard negative reports, such as enrollment dropping, and they were having little success with fundraising." Tom, who was also on the board of Franciscan University, mentioned to his fellow board members at CUA that Franciscan had an increase in enrollment each year and that their scores went up each year, "even though they had little money, were in a dying steel town, and didn't have sports teams." These were not home truths that the CUA board cared to contemplate. "They didn't like hearing that," Tom recalled. CUA's president dismissed the comparison, telling Tom that he was "comparing apples and oranges."

While on vacation in around 1993, Tom stepped into a Catholic bookstore and came across an anonymously authored book entitled *D.O.A.* ("dead on arrival"), in which the author, writing under the pseudonym "Catholicus," critiques those modernist theologians who were seeking to derail the recently published *Catechism of the Catholic Church*. As Tom thumbed through its pages, he noted to his annoyance that several of the dissident theologians responsible for attacking the *Catechism* were on the faculty at CUA: "Apparently, there were meetings at CUA with a group of CUA theologians leading the way to resist and derail the new catechism. This appalled me. How could this be happening at CUA, the bishops' university, right under the nose of the board of directors? I now felt that there was a reason I was on the board of CUA." Tom bought the book and, through some diligent research, discovered that its author was Kenneth D. Whitehead, a tireless defender of the Church who had served as an assistant secretary of education in the Reagan administration.

Apart from his desire as a bona fide Catholic to defend the Church from heterodoxy, Tom also had a purely personal reason for wishing to counter the influence of those modernists at CUA and elsewhere who were trying to undermine the newly published *Catechism*. He had met

with Cardinal Ratzinger several years earlier and had agreed
to fund the start-up costs of putting together a staff and
office to create the new catechism. Agreeing with Ratzinger
that the *Catechism* was urgently needed by the Church,
Tom was honored to be asked by the future pope to help:

> They were having a hard time getting it off the
> ground. And they needed seed money to hire staff
> and for other things to get it going. And whatever
> they asked for, I gave them. I have no idea how
> much, probably less than a million but more than
> one hundred thousand dollars. It was a pretty hum-
> ble operation, so a hundred thousand, a couple of
> hundred thousand really went a long way to help get
> them going. This was a great investment on my part.
> Millions of copies have been sold. It is a major tool
> in the revitalizing of the Church.

There can be no doubt that Tom's effusiveness is justified.
Indeed, if he had achieved nothing else whatsoever with
all of his wealth, his crucial role in the funding of the *Catechism* would be more than enough to earn the gratitude of
all those worldwide who have benefited from its publication and to all who rejoice in the renewal of the Church to
which its publication has contributed so powerfully.

Having helped to transform Fr. Gabriel Richard High
School into what he called "probably the most authentically
Catholic high school in the State of Michigan," Tom had
high hopes that he could have the same impact at CUA.
The first step was to inform his fellow CUA board mem-
bers of the activities of the dissident members of CUA's

theology department, especially with regard to their efforts to undermine the new *Catechism*. He approached Bishop Myers of Peoria who referred him to another bishop, a theologian, who wrote a report for Tom on the heterodoxy emanating from CUA's theology department. Tom sent this report to all members of the board, meeting opposition from the university's president and angering Cardinal Law, the chairman of the CUA board, who "had a few choice words for me." In contrast, Tom received support from Archbishop Chaput, who at the time was bishop of Rapid City, and from Cardinal Levada, who, at that time, was archbishop of Portland (Oregon). Cardinal Levada warned Tom that his courage would be sorely tested after what he'd stirred up.

Tom tried to get the issue placed on the agenda at the next board meeting but was told by Cardinal Law that the agenda was already full. Undaunted, Tom's persistence finally paid dividends when Cardinal Law reluctantly agreed that the issue could be discussed at the board's next three-day retreat, a concession that Tom considered "a victory."

This was, however, only the beginning. Overcoming his timidity in the presence of the members of the hierarchy on the CUA's board, he became increasingly outspoken. When names were proposed for possible commencement speakers or as potential recipients of honorary degrees, Tom would ask whether the candidates were practicing Catholics or whether they were pro-life. "Invariably, they didn't know. Instead of going through the rest of their list of candidates, they stopped and said they'd go back and get more information on them before proposing them. I said that this is the highest honor we give. There are many heroic Catholics out there. The other Catholic schools are ignoring them. Let's live up to our name, *Catholic* University, and focus on honoring committed Catholics who are pro-life also."

At the board's three-day retreat, Cardinal Law recommended that a special committee be set up to assess the Catholic identity of CUA. Bishop George, later to become archbishop of Chicago and to be made a cardinal by St. John Paul II, was named as chairman. "Cardinal Law said to me after the meeting that I should be very happy," Tom recalls. "I said I was *very* happy." There were, however, many who were very unhappy at Tom's efforts to get Catholic University to live up to its name. He had become a nuisance to the lukewarm and indifferent members of the board, and to the heretics on the faculty, he had become an irritating thorn in their side. Angered by what they considered unwanted and unwarranted meddling, they were moved to act against him when Tom's membership on the board came up for renewal. "There were three of us up for renewal, me, another layman, and a nun who no longer wore a habit. We were asked to leave the room. The votes were taken. When we came back into the room, I found that the other two were renewed and I was dropped." Tom was told that Cardinal Bevilacqua, the archbishop of Philadelphia and one of the most senior members of the hierarchy present, was very upset by the board's decision and spoke out against it, but to no avail.

If the liberal and lukewarm Catholics on the board had won a victory in their removal of Tom from their number, it was to prove short-lived. Brother Patrick Ellis, the CUA's president, who had taken over from Fr. Byron in 1992, was himself replaced by the more robustly orthodox Fr. David O'Connell in 1998. Fr. O'Connell would oversee the transformation, or transfiguration, of CUA into a far more authentically Catholic school during his twelve years at the helm. Shortly after Tom Monaghan's departure, many of the most egregious modernists in CUA's theology department had also departed, ushered out by the new spirit of orthodoxy. Today, Catholic University of America is the largest school in the list of authentic Catholic colleges and universities listed in the prestigious *Newman Guide to Choosing a Catholic College,* a status that it would hardly have merited in the early 1990s when Tom began agitating for authentic Catholic renewal. Did his pioneering efforts pave the way for this giant leap in the right direction? "It had to," he says. "No one else lifted a finger." And yet, with customary self-effacement, he adds that "it doesn't make any difference who gets the credit. It's the benefit to Catholic higher education which is significant."

Having witnessed how many nominally Catholic schools were "dropping the ball," Tom decided it was time to bring his own ball into play, using his money to found new schools or to renew existing ones. Apart from his success in helping to transform Fr. Gabriel Richard High School into one of the best Catholic schools in Michigan, he also saved another floundering school in the Ann Arbor area, St. Michael's Academy, which was a private Catholic school.

Tom helped initially by hiring a new principal, changing its name to Spiritus Sanctus Academy, and financing the construction of a new school building. He also brought in a new order of religious sisters to run the school, a decision that would providentially bestow a multitude of blessings on Tom, on the sisters, and on the Church in general.

The Dominican Sisters of Mary, Mother of the Eucharist was founded by Mother Mary Assumpta Long and three other sisters from Nashville, Tennessee, in early 1997. In Mother Assumpta's view, their meeting with Tom during the previous summer was providential. In an effort to discern God's will with regard to their plans to establish a new religious order, the four sisters were on their way to New York for a meeting with Cardinal O'Connor. Stopping for gas in Ann Arbor, they spotted an article on Tom in a local newspaper, his photograph catching their eye. Mother Assumpta knew Tom because she had previously given a talk at his invitation at Domino's Farms. On the spur of the moment, they decided to pay him a visit, hoping that they would find him available to meet with them.

"Of course, God had this planned all along," says Mother Assumpta. "We didn't have this planned. We didn't know what we were doing. When Tom Monaghan heard we were forming a community, God put it in his heart to help us."

Apart from inviting the sisters to run the school in Ann Arbor, Tom also became the order's chief benefactor, giving them fifteen million dollars and a large swathe of land on the north side of Ann Arbor on which the sisters built their motherhouse and paying their expenses for ten years.

Today, twenty years later, the order is one of the fastest growing in the United States. From the original four sisters, whom Tom took under his wing in 1997, the Dominican Sisters of Mary, Mother of the Eucharist now has more than 120 sisters. The average age of the sisters is only thirty, and the average age of those entering the order is twenty-one. Apart from the two Spiritus Sanctus Academies in the Ann Arbor area, which the sisters still run, they also teach in seventeen other schools in nine states, from Michigan to California. Although Tom would not wish to take the credit for this astonishing success story, which has more to do with the faith and charism of the sisters and the working of the Holy Spirit, he deserves great credit for his important role in helping the sisters get established.

In addition to his financial commitment to the newly founded Dominican Sisters of Mary, Mother of the Eucharist, Tom was donating substantial sums of money to pro-life political candidates and was still providing financial support for Legatus. He was, however, keen to do more, as evidenced by his ambitious plans to start a new Catholic college and law school. The problem was that his multifarious philanthropic endeavors had to comply with the strictures placed upon him by Morgan Bank during the refinancing of Domino's in 1994. These strictures restricted his charitable donations to his foundation or other charities to no more than 10 percent of the company's profits. Thankfully, by 1998, it was clear that Domino's was not only surviving in the pizza wars but positively thriving. Although Pizza Hut retained its market dominance, with 22 percent of the US market, Domino's was holding its own in terms of sales, enjoying almost 12 percent of the market, ahead of Little Caesars' 8 percent and Papa John's 4 percent. More to the point, Domino's market share had actually increased over the previous four years, whereas Pizza Hut and Little Caesars were both losing ground. Domino's had 31 percent of the delivery market, compared to Pizza Hut's 20 percent. Even more impressive was the growth in global sales, which had risen from $2.2 billion in 1993 to $3.2 billion in 1997, an upturn in fortunes that reflected Domino's successful metamorphosis into a fully fledged multinational corporation, no longer dependent solely on the volatile US pizza market. It was, therefore, a confident Tom Monaghan who was profiled in *Time* magazine on October 26, 1998, a few weeks after he had surprised the business world by selling 92.5 percent of his stake in Domino's to Bain Capital, a private investment firm, for an estimated $1 billion. Approximately five years later, Tom would sell his remaining interest in the company.

The *Time* profile, entitled "A Tale of Pizza, Pride and Piety," reflected the way that the wider world perceived Tom Monaghan as he bowed out of the pizza wars in pursuit of higher things. "Domino's founder Tom Monaghan, 61, has always been a larger-than-life contradiction," the article begins. "He made a fortune pioneering a no-frills pizza delivery business, then nearly squandered it on his own ostentatious life-style." Mentioning his struggles over the previous decade to rebuild the apparently floundering Domino's empire, the article refers to his success in selling the company for such a large sum of money. There could be little doubt that Tom was quitting while he was winning.

"The sale marked the end of one of the most colorful and controversial stewardships of a pizza company—or for that matter any other type of business," the article continues. Describing Tom as "a devout Roman Catholic and antiabortion campaigner," the profile discusses his passion for "charitable pursuits at home and in foreign countries," listing his opening of a mission in Honduras and the construction of the cathedral in Nicaragua, as well as his founding of Catholic schools in Ann Arbor and a new Catholic liberal arts college in nearby Ypsilanti, the latter being an allusion to the embryonic entity that would grow over the next decade into Ave Maria University. The article also quotes Tom's daughter, Maggie, stating that her father "loves his charities" and that he "wanted to leave [Domino's] before he becomes too old to enjoy the benefits of his charity work."

"Monaghan was long known more for self-indulgence than for selflessness," the *Time* profile continues, listing his amassing of a "gaudy mix of Bugatti autos, Frank Lloyd Wright drawings and artifacts, and a dream ranch in Ann Arbor where herds of buffalo roamed."

> Monaghan explained these sprees as compensation for the fact that his mother abandoned him at the age of four to foster homes and an orphanage. As owner of the Detroit Tigers, he liked to swoop down on home games in his helicopter. He once considered building a 35-story slanted tower dubbed—what else?—the Leaning Tower of Pizza.
>
> Yet none of those extravagances really made him happy. So in 1989 Monaghan took a one and

a half year leave from Domino's to devote himself to Catholic charities and soon began to dump his toys. . . . "Most of the time I was buying things to get attention, to have people notice me," Monaghan once remarked. "That's the sin of pride, the worst sin of all, and I'm the guiltiest person."

Paying due attention to the centrality of the Christian faith in Tom's life, without the sneering undertone that so often accompanied any discussion of his Catholic beliefs in the media, the *Time* profile mentioned Tom's childhood dreams of becoming a priest and an architect and listed C. S. Lewis's *Mere Christianity* as the preeminent influence on his change of outlook, especially with regard to the way he viewed his wealth and possessions, highlighting his plans to "die broke." All in all, *Time* had summarized Tom's life and legacy, and his conversion of heart, with a refreshing fairness. It was a fitting tribute to the "larger-than-life contradiction," the scarred and bruised veteran of the pizza wars who was retiring from the commercial fray as a winner who could wear his many business victories like medals of honor on his chest. More to the point, he now had a billion dollars, the spoils of war, to arm those fighting in a very different war. Henceforth, he would devote his energy and his money to fighting the culture wars, helping those engaged in the battle for souls in an increasingly hostile world, and having been inspired by the success of Franciscan University and having experienced the problems at Catholic University of America, he set his primary goal as the winning of souls through the promotion of education as if truth mattered.

CHAPTER 15

SOWING SEEDS

D ESIRING TO "die broke" and with his new fortune to spend, Tom surveyed his options. Having been approached and solicited by numerous Catholic charities and projects over the years, he had a pretty good vision of where his money could most help the building of the Church in the United States. "I had narrowed it down to the two most important categories: Catholic education and Catholic media."

He was highly impressed with the "outstanding job" that Mother Angelica had done with the Eternal Word Television Network (EWTN) and was keen to work with her in the building of Catholic radio. EWTN already had the programming, which was one of the biggest costs of operating a radio station, and Mother Angelica was offering to make it available to any entrepreneurial spirits who wanted to start a local Catholic radio station. "We were the first to take her up on her offer," says Tom. Starting modestly with a small rented station in Ann Arbor/Ypsilanti, Ave Maria Radio first went on the air on September 6, 1996. At the end of 1998, following the sale of Domino's, Tom was able to invest much more money in what he called "this important apostolate."

There were, in the 1990s, well over a thousand Protestant radio stations, whereas Ave Maria, when it was launched, was the only Catholic radio station in the country. Considering the number of Catholics in the United States, this particular apostolate was clearly being woefully neglected. Tom set about putting this right. He had already hired Al Kresta, a well-known talk-show personality, to run the radio station. In the 1980s and early 1990s, Kresta, then a Protestant pastor, hosted "Talk From the Heart," one of the top-rated Christian talk programs on WMUZ. After Kresta had converted to Catholicism, Tom saw him speaking at a local meeting and was immediately impressed. "This is the Catholic Rush Limbaugh," he said to himself. With Kresta at the helm, Ave Maria Radio began to move forward by leaps and bounds. The studio was moved to custom-built premises at Domino's Farms, two other stations were added, and the station began producing its own shows in addition to those it was broadcasting under license from EWTN. Soon, Ave Maria Radio was producing six hours of Catholic programming per day. Ten years later, Al Kresta's program was being aired on about 120 of the 140 or so Catholic radio stations across the country. Tom continues to listen to "Kresta in the Afternoon," and he is as impressed today as when he first heard Kresta speak more than twenty years ago. "I don't know who would be more educated. He can talk on anybody's level—he has approximately thirty-five thousand books in his personal home."

By the end of 2015, with Al Kresta still serving as its president and CEO, Ave Maria Radio's prime-time offerings were being broadcast in over 320 markets throughout the United States. This explosion in Catholic radio is nothing short of a media revolution, for which Tom deserves a place of honor as a blazing pioneer, second only to Mother Angelica, of whom he remains a loyal disciple. "I believe Mother Angelica has brought more people into the Church and back to the Church than any one person in history," he says.

Another initiative that Tom got involved with (taking it over and changing its name), and one that is all too often forgotten in the long litany of initiatives he has launched over the years, is Ave Maria Singles, a Catholic matchmaking agency that, by 2015, had brought together more than two thousand couples into holy wedlock. Considering that these married couples are likely to follow the Church's teaching and be open to the gift of life, it is not unreasonable to estimate that Tom's fathering of Ave Maria Singles had led to his being the de facto godfather to almost ten thousand children, the vast majority of whom are being brought up in the practice of the Faith!

Meanwhile Tom's work with Legatus, the organization for Catholic CEOs and business leaders, which he'd founded in 1987, continued apace. In October 1998, a month after the sale of Domino's, he was part of the Legatus pilgrimage to Rome, meeting Pope John Paul II and future pope Cardinal Ratzinger at the Vatican. By the end of the year, Legatus had 1,200 members in twenty-two chapters throughout the United States and beyond. New chapters had been started in Las Vegas and Chicago in 1998, with further new chapters starting in 1999 in Dallas, Miami, Grand Rapids, Orange County, San Diego, and Cleveland. In December 1999, Legatus launched its website, legatus.org. Tom's own annual contribution to Legatus in 1998 was three million dollars, a fivefold increase on his contribution five years earlier, but the organization's impressive growth warranted the increased investment on his part. Today, Legatus has some ninety chapters and 2,600 members.

Tom's main preoccupation was, however, in the area of Catholic higher education. With his hands freed from any involvement in the pizza business, he was now at liberty to unleash all his considerable energy on the various educational projects that he'd launched in the previous year or two. In the fall of 1997, he opened the Ave Maria Institute in Ypsilanti, Michigan, a Catholic undergraduate liberal arts institution, which would evolve into Ave Maria University. Beginning with only ten students and three professors, and unable to call itself a college under Michigan state law because it was not yet fully accredited, it had an inauspicious enough start. It would, however, grow exponentially when it became one of Tom's main priorities, though not without considerable growing pains, as we shall see.

Not surprisingly, considering Tom's positive experience of Franciscan University of Steubenville and his admiration for its charismatic president, Fr. Michael Scanlan, he originally planned to model his own embryonic university on the curriculum and educational philosophy of FUS. He sought and followed the advice of

Nick Healy, FUS's vice-president for development, and Michael Healy, FUS's provost, and at the latter's suggestion, he approached Ron Muller, a professor of philosophy who had taught at the University of Dallas and had cofounded Thomas More College in Fort Worth, to serve as Ave Maria Institute's first provost.

Having sought and received the blessing of Bishop Mengeling, the newly appointed bishop of Lansing, the Ave Maria Institute was ready to open its doors to students. Ironically, however, it found itself initially homeless in spite of the fact that Tom owned 1,700 acres on the edge of Ann Arbor where Domino's Farms, Domino's corporate headquarters, is located. "We had been accumulating this land for many years with the vague idea it would be used to serve the Church," Tom explains. Twenty acres had been allotted to Mother Assumpta and her new order of Dominican sisters, forty acres for Fr. Gabriel Richard High School, and around eight acres for Christ the King Parish. Ten acres had been used to build Spiritus Sanctus Academy, and a further ten acres had been made available to a group of Maronite priests from Lebanon who said Mass and heard confessions at the chapel at Domino's Farms. After the sale of Domino's, Tom envisaged that the largest part of the property would be used for the campus of the planned university. However, this would not be possible until the Ann Arbor Township Board agreed to rezone the property. Since the board was composed, for the most part, of individuals who seemed not to want to understand his motives, Tom was expecting a difficult and uphill struggle that would take some time. In the meantime, he needed somewhere to serve as a temporary campus for the ten students who had registered for the Ave Maria Institute's inaugural year.

"We had to find a building to get started in," Tom remembers. "We found an abandoned elementary school in Ypsilanti, adjacent to Eastern Michigan University, on about five acres of land. The school board was auctioning it off. We were the only bidder at about $500,000, but they didn't want to sell it to us. Finally we made a deal to buy it for $550,000 with the understanding it would not be a charter school, which was their biggest fear."

There was something romantically ironic or perhaps even beautifully providential about the location of the new "institute," which within a year would receive permission from the state to call itself a college. It was located only a stone's throw from the first pizza store that, almost forty years earlier, Tom had opened in partnership with his brother. It was certainly singularly apt that Tom's new life as a full-time Catholic benefactor should be located on almost the same spot that his old life as a pizza entrepreneur had begun.

Parallel with Tom's efforts to revitalize Catholic education in the United States were efforts to provide a good Catholic education for the poor in Central America. He had already helped to build a mission in Honduras, providing funding for a clinic and a pharmacy, as well as helping to found self-sustaining farms and businesses, and had paid $3.5 million toward the building of a new cathedral in Nicaragua. In 1998, he turned his attention to building schools, opening the Espiritu Santo grammar school for the poor in Zacapa, an agricultural region of Honduras.

The school cost $150,000 to build and required a further $130,000 per year in operating costs. In order to ensure that the poorest children could attend, Tom established Ave Maria Missions to underwrite tuition for those unable to pay.

A couple of years later, in July of 2000, Ave Maria College would buy a small liberal arts school in San Marcos, Nicaragua, from the University of Mobile. Initially, Tom had been reluctant to support such an investment of money in the project but was persuaded by Cardinal Obando y Bravo that it was imperative that the campus, which was the only US accredited institution of higher education in Central America, be kept open. "I resisted," Tom remembers. "I really didn't want to do it. Reluctantly, I agreed to fly down there, and it was clear that the Cardinal really wanted me to keep the college open. I thought that perhaps it was God's will that I did so." The institution was renamed the Ave Maria College of the Americas, echoing the name of the new college in Michigan, and efforts would be made over the years to integrate the vision and needs of the two institutions, with limited success.

In the fall of 1998, Tom set in motion plans for building a Catholic law school and a Catholic public interest law center. His reasoning was simple enough. "Law is such an important profession. It is lawyers who effectively run our country. They have so much influence on our society. Most of our politicians are lawyers, of course all our judges are lawyers. Every large corporation has lawyers at every board meeting, if not on the board. Since this is so, it's very important that future lawyers are trained in ethics."

In the midnineties, while Tom was serving on the board of Franciscan University, the idea of a new Catholic law school had been proposed and studied. Due to costs, the Franciscan University board never pursued the idea, but it remained in the back of Tom's mind. It was, however, the firing of five professors at the University of Detroit Mercy School of Law that prompted him to act at this time. "The idea of actually founding a law school came to my mind when I read about the five law professors," Tom says. "I was told that they were fired because they were orthodox."

In point of fact the five professors—Joseph Falvey, Laura Hirschfeld, Mollie Murphy, Richard Myers and Stephen Safranek—were fired because they had the courage to protest publicly against the law school's decision to invite the Michigan Supreme Court chief justice, who had written decisions upholding abortion and euthanasia, to speak at the law school's annual "Red Mass," at which, ironically, the school publicly professed its commitment to its Catholic principles. The five courageous professors had asked the administration to reconsider its invitation to someone who had publicly contravened the Catholic Church's position on the sanctity and dignity of human life. When the administration refused to rescind the invitation the professors demonstrated outside the Mass, an act of freedom of expression that the Jesuits and Sisters of Mercy who ran the school considered a crime warranting the professors' dismissal from the faculty.

For Tom, who had witnessed such heterodox shenanigans at the Catholic University of America, this persecution of bona fide Catholics by modernists acting in bad

faith could not go unanswered. Initially, he asked Charles
Rice, a well-known and respected professor of law at Notre
Dame Law School, to serve as the first dean of the proposed new law school. Tom trusted Rice, whom he knew
from their both being members of the governing board at
Franciscan University. Rice had a hard-earned reputation
as a courageous defender of orthodoxy and as an outspoken
pro-life advocate. The fact that he had served in the US
Marine Corps and had risen to the rank of lieutenant colonel in the USMC Reserve would no doubt have reinforced
Tom's high opinion of him, as would the fact that he served
as an assistant coach of the Notre Dame Boxing Club. In
short and in sum, Charles Rice was a tried and tested culture warrior of the first order who, in the culture wars that
Tom was now fighting, had everything needed to serve as
dean of his law school. Rice declined on the grounds that,
at sixty-seven, he was too old. He did, however, agree to
serve as a member of the school's founding board of gover-
nors, and to teach as a visiting professor. He suggested that
Tom approach Bernie Dobranski, dean of the law school at
Catholic University of America, to be the dean.

   Tom already knew Dobranski. "I knew him from when
I was on the board of Catholic University. He was hired
away from the University of Detroit Mercy while I was on
CUA's board. Later, when I was on the search committee
for a new president for CUA, his name was mentioned as
a candidate." Furthermore, the "Fired Five" whom Tom
hoped to hire as the inaugural faculty of his law school,
told him that it was "essential" that Dobranski was persuaded to come on board.

"I called Bernie," Tom recalled. "Apparently Rice had talked to him about it. He was interested." The two men met in Ann Arbor. Tom told Dobranski of his plan to hire the five law professors fired by the University of Detroit Mercy School of Law, explaining that they had given him the impression that the new law school could open in the fall of 1999, in less than a year. Furthermore, they were confident that they could bring many of their former students with them, thereby providing a ready-made faculty and student body. It all seemed too good to be true. According to Dobranski, it was indeed too good to be true, or at least too good to be feasible. Dobranski was interested in taking the new position, but he was insistent that the fall of 2000 was the earliest that the school could open. Tom baulked at the extra year but was convinced that Dobranski was the man for the job and that he needed to trust his judgment.

> It didn't take long to strike a deal. Bernie was giving up a secure situation for a rather risky one. But he was a man of vision and could see the potential of a new type of law school. He told me that we should do it the right way right from the beginning; otherwise, it'd take years to improve the image to where we'd want it to be. What we eventually wanted was the best Catholic law school in the country. He had a clear vision of what he wanted and what it would take. I enthusiastically bought the idea. A contract was signed and we were off.

Joseph Falvey, one of the "Fired Five," was named associate dean and was made responsible for much of the preliminary groundwork under Dobranski's direction and oversight while the latter was finishing up at Catholic University of America. In the interim, efforts were being made at CUA to try to talk Dobranski out of leaving. After the president of CUA had tried and failed, Cardinal Law did his best to persuade Dobranski to stay. His failure to do so put an additional strain on the Cardinal's relationship with Tom, its having been tested already because of Tom's outspokenness when he was on the CUA's board. "I had known Cardinal Law for some time. He's the one who got me started on the Nicaragua Cathedral project. He had used my jet a number of times. I helped fund his Cambridge Institute, an orthodox Catholic think tank." None of this mattered, or apparently had been forgotten, as Cardinal Law vented his fury on Tom. "He literally chewed me out and tongue-lashed me," Tom remembers, demanding to know how Tom had dared to "steal" Dobranski from "the Bishops' University." Tom sat in silence, taking the verbal abuse on the proverbial chin. Finally, when a lull in the tirade enabled him to speak, Tom told Cardinal Law that he simply believed he was doing God's will.

With Dobranski on board and "a ready-made faculty" of committed law professors who had already made great sacrifices for the Faith, Tom proceeded with his plans to launch Ave Maria School of Law. A building in Ann Arbor was bought as an interim campus until such time as Domino's Farms was rezoned, at which point the law school would be relocated, along with Ave Maria College, to a new permanent site on the land around the Domino's corporate headquarters. There were, however, growing pains, even at these early stages, which would be destined to cause major problems a few years later. Tom had agreed in the earliest planning stages that the law school should be kept separate from the college. "Ave Maria College was a rather humble operation, while with the law school, we were going first-class from the beginning with a much larger budget. I had no problem with this as long as it had the same name and was on the same campus."

Declaring himself "a great believer in decentralization," a fact that was readily demonstrable from the way that he'd structured Domino's and the manner in which he'd trusted his executives and franchisees at Domino's to run things within their spheres of responsibility without the need for micromanagement, he believed that the separation of the law school from the college "might even have some advantages." The problem was that his view of separation was not necessarily in harmony with that envisaged by the founding faculty of the law school, or, for that matter, the faculty of the college. Tom saw the law school as being or at least becoming "the flagship of Ave Maria College, eventually Ave Maria University." In contrast, many at the law school were more interested in waving flags of independence from the college than in serving as a flagship of it, and some of the faculty at the college were opposed to its ever becoming a university of any sort, with or without a law school. Even as Tom was sowing seeds of Catholic renewal, investing his money in authentic Catholic education, seeds of discord were being sown, the weeds among the wheat, which would cause a shadow to fall over his high hopes and best-laid schemes.

CHAPTER 16

A SHADOW FALLS

Between the idea
And the reality
Between the motion
And the act
Falls the Shadow . . .
Between the conception
And the creation . . .
Between the potency
And the existence
Falls the Shadow . . .

T. S. Eliot

WHEN TOM described the launching of the Ave Maria School of Law as a "first-class" operation, he was not exaggerating. "We had an outstanding board. We put together a dream list and almost everyone we asked accepted." There were "several brainstorming meetings with top Catholic legal people, including Supreme Court Justice Scalia, who flew out to Ann Arbor to spend a whole day meeting with us about the curriculum and other matters pertinent to the formation of this new authentically Catholic law school." The board that was assembled represented a veritable who's who of top names in the Church and the legal profession, which Tom described as "the most impressive, talented board I've ever been on." Apart from Bernard Dobranski and Tom himself, the other members of the founding board included Helen Alvaré, who worked in the pro-life office at the National Conference of Catholic Bishops; Gerard Bradley, professor of law at the University of Notre Dame; Archbishop Charles Chaput, then archbishop of Denver; the Honorable William Clark, former US secretary of the interior under President Regan; Fr. Joseph Fessio, founder and editor of Ignatius Press; Robert George, holder of the McCormick Chair in Jurisprudence at Princeton; Representative Henry Hyde, US congressman from the Sixth District of Illinois; Adam Cardinal Maida, archbishop of Detroit (an attorney); John Cardinal O'Connor, archbishop of New York; Charles Rice, professor of law at the University of Notre Dame; the Honorable James Ryan, judge of the US Court of Appeals for the Sixth Circuit; and Fr. Michael Scanlan (an attorney), president of Franciscan University of Steubenville. As if such an assembly of dignitaries were not enough, the "biggest coup" in Tom's estimation was getting Judge Robert Bork to agree to serve on the faculty.

Having assembled such an illustrious board, the curtain was raised on the Ave Maria School of Law in November 1999, at Ann Arbor's Crowne Plaza Hotel, when Supreme Court Justice Clarence Thomas delivered the inaugural lecture before an invited audience of 250 lawyers and other guests. After the lecture, Thomas took Tom and Dean Dobranski to one side and told them that they were doing something "very, very important" and then, raising his voice, announced to everyone in the room that "my hat's off to this endeavor."

Parallel with his work on the founding of the Ave Maria School of Law, Tom was helping to establish the Thomas More Law Center, which was endeavoring to preserve and protect the Christian ethical foundations of American culture. In the years ahead, the TMLC, under the presidency of Richard Thompson, would serve as a Christian antidote to the secularist American Civil Liberties Union, taking up cases, free of charge, to defend religious freedom, time-honored family values, and the dignity and sanctity of human life. In the first years of operation, before it found its feet financially, Tom covered the TMLC's annual deficit, which was $570,000 in its first year and rose at one point to a high of $1.375 million a year. Tom's seed money and subsequent support were described by Thompson as being "indispensable" to the TMLC's ability to survive and then thrive. In fact, Thompson, who was already doing some work for Tom during the unrest at University of Detroit Mercy School of Law, was instrumental in helping to bring the "Fired Five" together with Tom. He served as the point of contact in the early days of the formation of the law school until Dobranski and the others were hired.

Meanwhile, as the law school was taking "first-class" shape in Ann Arbor, attracting a host of celebrities, Ave Maria College, the "humble operation" in neighboring Ypsilanti, was quietly making progress. Nick Healy, who had recently left his position at Franciscan University, became AMC's first president. Nick came aboard as the college prepared to take the next steps toward becoming a university and as it took over the international campus in Nicaragua from the University of Mobile. The interim campus was expanded through the purchase of adjoining buildings on the same block, including a few houses and a couple of apartment buildings. The latter were intended as makeshift dormitories, which, as yet, were mostly empty because AMC only had eighteen students. Addressing the urgent need for new students, Tom approached his friend Ralph Martin, whose apostolate, Renewal Ministries, had many connections in Eastern Europe as a consequence of its mission work there in the wake of the fall of communism. Tom offered to donate two thousand dollars to Renewal Ministries for every student from Eastern Europe that Martin and his colleagues recruited for the college. Within a year, 25 percent of AMC's students were from Slovakia, Poland, or the Ukraine, all of whom were receiving a full ride. Since these students were usually handpicked by their local bishops, they were of exceptional quality, ensuring that AMC's SAT scores were exceptionally high for a new school.

In spite of Tom having bought up most of the buildings on the block, it was evident that the location in Ypsilanti would not be adequate for very long if the college expanded into a fully fledged university as was hoped and envisaged. It was, therefore, important that planning permission was obtained to build on the space available at Domino's Farms. In 2001, Ave Maria College formally presented detailed plans to the Ann Arbor Township Board, requesting that the board rezone Domino's Farms to permit the construction of a university campus with classrooms, dormitories, and administration buildings. As this was done, Tom and the board of the college could not have been very confident of success. The relationship between Domino's Farms and the township had been rocky over the years, and this was a change in direction that required their approval:

> I just wanted to be treated fairly. For years, the board seemed opposed to us and seemed to treat us as an enemy. We are the largest taxpayer by far in the township, obeying the law, taking very good care of our buildings, and we were treated like the enemy. It seemed every request we made was turned down. For example, we were forbidden to do our light show at Christmastime. We sued and we won. We asked to change our sign, which had changing letters to announce our events in the building. We wanted it to be electronic so we could do it automatically instead of manually. We were turned down. We sued and they ended up conceding most of what we wanted before it went to court. The township put up a cell phone tower next to our property, which was an eyesore, near our building. Again we sued, but lost. They refused to let us put a farmer's market on our property next to our petting farm; this time, with the advice of an attorney, we decided not to sue—a mistake. We tried to set up a retreat facility.

> Again they refused. Again we sued. We won and they
> appealed and lost.

It took nine months for the township board to formally reject the request for rezoning. While one might understand the desire of the board to keep the rural feel of this gem of a township, the bigger picture seems not to have been addressed. Not only did the plans call for responsible development of Tom's land, but they would also have brought hundreds of millions of dollars to a hurting Michigan economy: not only construction jobs but a host of new jobs associated with a start-up university. Since such musings are beyond the scope of this book, we will move on.

At the beginning of the fall semester in 2001, the number of students enrolled at Ave Maria College had increased to over seventy, with seventeen faculty members to teach them. The present author was one of the new faculty members hired that year, arriving from his native England to take up the position of writer-in-residence and associate professor of literature. He recalls that radical differences already existed between some members of the faculty and the college's administration. A significant section of the faculty were wedded to the idea of the college remaining a small, integrated liberal arts institution, similar to existing schools such as Christendom College in Virginia, that would offer only a handful of majors, none of which would be in the physical or social sciences, and would not grow in size beyond a few hundred students. This vision was radically different from that envisaged by Tom; by Nick

Healy, AMC's president; or by the AMC board of trustees. Healy insists,

> From the beginning, it was my idea, which Tom strongly supported—or it was Tom's idea, which I strongly supported?—that the college was the kernel of what would be a full-blown university. It was never intended by us to be a small Catholic enclave, but there were some there who thought that's what it should be. The first provost would've preferred a small liberal arts college. But I knew that Tom thought that a university was needed, and I agree. There's already a number of small Catholic colleges across the country, but there's no full-blown Catholic university that shares the commitment to the faith that Ave Maria has.

There's no doubt that, objectively speaking, Healy's memory of the situation accords with the facts. The idea of starting the college had as its genesis a desire on Tom's part to emulate the success of Franciscan University. "An organization was set up to try to get other FUS-type schools started around the world," says Tom. "I believe Nick Healy initiated the idea, as he did many ideas. An entity called Christus Magister was set up by FUS to help start up these new schools. I was asked to be on the board. I immediately volunteered to start the first school."

The problem was that this vision, shared by AMC's founder and its president, was not communicated very effectively, or at all, to the college's faculty, many of whom were under the impression, or illusion, that they had the authority to forge the college's vision and curriculum. Many faculty meetings were spent in 2001 and 2002 arguing over the philosophy of the curriculum, including, on occasion, interminable discussions on relative minutiae. It was as though a dozen or so minds were trying to impose their will on this new institution, seeing it as a tabula rasa on which they could write their own agendas, endeavoring to make Ave Maria College the perfect school, better than all others. The whole process was becoming dangerously utopian.

Nick Healy perceived clearly this utopian dimension. "People who are academics build their whole vocation around an academic life. Suddenly there's a new academic institution that maybe is going to be the ideal which they longed for. They get invested in it in a very unwholesome way, not seeing that [not only is] every institution flawed but every human being is flawed. Problems arise when the vision doesn't turn out quite as they wanted. The reaction is one of extreme dismay." This is true, and all very well, but part of the problem in the early days of Ave Maria College was that the faculty were never told very clearly what the vision of the college actually was. It was in the absence of a clearly enunciated vision that people began to believe in the practical attainability of their own visions of what the college should be. Believing that AMC was there for the taking or the making, many members of the faculty believed that they would be able to mold the institution into their own idealized image of a perfect Catholic school.

There was a sense of enmity and resentment on the part of many faculty members toward the college's administration, which was seen as being ignorant and ill-qualified to make decisions concerning the academic nature of the institution. The two visions—that of Tom, Nick Healy, and the board on the one hand and that of the liberal arts purists on the other—were ultimately at loggerheads and irreconcilable. It was, therefore, only a matter of time before the two forces collided. Tensions were raised in 2002 when new disciplines were added to the curriculum—such as biology, physics, and economics—that were not considered by the liberal arts purists to be an authentic part of a Catholic education. Unsurprisingly, the new faculty hired to teach these additional disciplines sided with the administration with regard to the broader vision of a university, as distinct from the narrower vision of the small liberal arts college, thereby raising tensions on the faculty and creating factions. With temperatures running high, it would only take a spark to ignite the various parties into open warfare. That spark was the decision to move the college's campus to Florida.

The decision to move to Florida was Tom's idea, but the college's board of trustees embraced it. "I realized we were getting nowhere with the township," he says. The Ann Arbor Township Board's interminable delay in reaching a decision was moving the operation of both the college and the law school into a crisis situation. Recruitment at the college was so successful it looked as though enrollment would jump from seventy to two hundred students in the coming year, a projection that would prove almost correct. Meanwhile, the law school had opened with three times the number of students that Tom or anyone else had expected. "We were hoping for twenty-five or so with an

LSAT average of about 153. We wound up with seventy-six students with an LSAT of 158, well into the top quartile! Never did a new law school start with such high student scores." This success was causing its own problems. "The law school and especially the college were bursting at the seams. I had figured we'd probably lose the zoning battle, but you can't get into court until they turn you down, and we'd certainly win in the court. Unfortunately, what I didn't figure was how long it'd take to get a vote of refusal so we could go to court."

With time running out before the makeshift campus at Ypsilanti reached capacity and with the likely rejection of the rezoning by the township leading to a long and drawn out legal battle, Tom felt that he was facing insurmountable obstacles. For once, he had no idea what he could or should do next. "I was thinking about the pickle I was in. I had no option left but to pray. I told Our Lady that I needed help. I couldn't do it myself."

Having put the matter into the hands of God, through the intercession of His Mother, he and Margie departed for their annual post-Christmas vacation in Naples, Florida, a place they'd discovered a few years earlier and had since enjoyed visiting regularly. It was during this visit to Florida's gulf coast in early 2002 that Tom had the vision of relocating the college and law school to this part of the country. It seemed to make so much sense. Florida was one of the fastest-growing states in the whole country, and the Naples area was the fastest-growing part of Florida. It would be the perfect place to attract students and faculty. Whereas 90 percent of Catholic schools were in the North or Northeast of the country, there were fewer than ten in the South and only three in Florida. He needn't waste any more time fighting the Ann Arbor Township Board. He would simply shake the Michigan dust from his feet and head south, taking the college and law school with him. It was the answer to prayer!

Returning from vacation, Tom met with Nick Healy and broached the idea of transitioning the college to a new location in Florida, changing its name to Ave Maria University in the process. Nick thought the idea truly inspired and offered to travel to Florida to lay the foundations for the move. He would seek a good location for the campus and meet with attorneys. Tom then took the idea to the college's board, which voted unanimously in favor of the move. All seemed to be going very smoothly until news of the move reached the faculty, some of whom were supportive and enthusiastic but many of whom greeted the news with disbelief and dismay. From this time on, the faculty divided into the pro-Florida and anti-Florida factions, with the latter group becoming more bitterly entrenched as the plans for the move began to take shape.

If the situation at the college was becoming ugly, it was overshadowed by the storm that was brewing at the law school. After the announcement of a feasibility study to examine the proposed move to Florida was made, a vociferous group of faculty members, led by a very persuasive board member, opposed the move. This board member wrote what Tom described as "a scathing criticism of the move," sending it to all members of the board. Tom was at the law school, on his way to meet Dean Dobranski to discuss this letter, when he bumped into the author in the hallway. "I was furious," Tom remembered. "I rarely get angry, or at least I rarely express my anger, but I did this time." The board member told Tom to relax and suggested that they go to the board room to continue the discussion in a more private setting. He went on to tell Tom that he was convinced that the law school would "disintegrate" if it moved to Florida. Tom responded by berating him for his lack of confidence in the law school's leadership.

The ensuing board meeting was something of a blood-bath. The dissident board member's bullheadedness created "a battlefield type of atmosphere," Tom recalls. He made a lot of charges that Tom considered "untrue" and hinted darkly of lawsuits if Tom attempted to force the law school to relocate to Florida. Tom was defended in the heat of the meeting by Fr. Fessio who took exception to the belliger-ent and ad hominem nature of the attacks. Responding to the various charges, Tom listed the benefits to be gained from a move to Florida. These included the fact that Naples was a fast-growing and very affluent area of the country and that there were no other law schools in the area, in con-trast to the law school's current location, only a few miles from the University of Michigan's prestigious law school and not too far from the University of Detroit Mercy School of Law and numerous other law schools within a one-hour drive. He pointed out that Naples probably had the highest average net worth per capita of anywhere in the United States and that many of these were Catholics and therefore potential donors. Tom also sought to con-vince the board of the benefits of the law school sharing a campus with the university and of his vision of Ave Maria University becoming a top Catholic school.

In an effort to convince the faculties at the college and the law school of the wisdom of the move to Florida, Tom financed trips to Naples for the faculty and their spouses. "It only made things worse," he recalled. "Every board meeting was a battleground." The opposition continued to send out reports attacking the Florida project before each meeting and would submit motions that fueled further heated debate. In the end, Tom made the ultimatum that he could not continue to put any more money into Ave Maria School of Law if it did not make the move to Florida. "I couldn't afford two campuses in different locations," he explained. "From the beginning, I put so much money into Ave Maria School of Law because it was to be the flagship for AMU. I could live with the fact it was a separate entity, as long as it had the same name and was on the same campus."

Years later, Tom still felt shocked and scarred by the sheer bitterness of the response to his desire to move AMU and AMSL to Florida. "I can understand why people didn't want to move," he says, "but I can't understand why it became so vicious. It could be that what we are doing could be one of the most important contributions to the Church. The devil knows that and wants to see it destroyed. Every great movement or institution in Church history had enormous difficulties in its early stages. Our difficulties could be a sign that we have tremendous potential for good."

Undaunted by the slings and arrows of outraged faculty, Tom continued to seek the silver lining to the dark storm cloud that had descended on his plans. Had he been more literarily minded, he might have mused with T. S. Eliot that a shadow falls between the idea and the reality and between the conception of a thing and its creation. He might have pondered, with Eliot, that there is a shadow that falls between a thing's potency, its potential, and its existence. He might have concluded that the shadow that falls is nothing less than the shadow of the Fall itself.

CHAPTER 17

GROWING PAINS

D URING THE summer of 2002, Nick Healy traveled to Florida to lay the groundwork for the moving
of the college and soon-to-be university to sunnier climes.
Later that year, he was joined by Fr. Fessio, who had been
hired as AMC's chancellor. Fessio was a feisty character
who had built a reputation as one who had the courage
of his orthodox convictions. He founded the St. Ignatius
Institute at the Jesuit-run University of San Francisco in
1976 as an oasis of Catholic orthodoxy in the desert of
indifference and heterodoxy that prevailed at USF, and two
years later, he founded Ignatius Press, a dynamically orthodox publishing house that would have a profound impact
on Catholic culture in the English-speaking world. In early
2001, he was fired from USF when his robust orthodoxy
became too much for the modernist ascendancy at the
university to handle. At the same time, the St. Ignatius
Institute was unceremoniously shut down. Never one to
resist a good fight when justice seemed to demand it, Fessio responded by founding Campion College in San Francisco, setting up a bastion of orthodoxy on USF's doorstep.

His Jesuit superiors responded to this show of chutzpah by exiling him to the small town of Duarte on the edge of the San Gabriel Mountains to serve as an assistant chaplain in a Catholic hospital, an act of crass bullying that caused outrage throughout the English-speaking Catholic world and allegedly angered Cardinal Ratzinger, who had served as Fessio's thesis director many years earlier and with whom he had retained a friendship. It was rumored that Ratzinger contacted the Jesuits' superior general in Rome who, in turn, instructed Fessio's superiors to allow him to join Ave Maria College as its chancellor when Tom made him the offer.

In offering Fessio a job shortly after his firing by a heterodox institution, Tom was following in what was becoming a noble tradition. Not only had he offered the "Fired Five" positions at the Ave Maria School of Law after they'd been dismissed by the University of Detroit Mercy for their pro-life stance, but he'd also established the Institute for Pastoral Theology, a master's program that was grafted onto Ave Maria University, to accommodate four faculty members at another Catholic university who had resigned in April 1999 because of what they considered theological backsliding at that institution. It seemed that Tom had established a sort of refugee program for orthodox academics who had been made homeless by the abandonment of orthodoxy by nominally Catholic universities.

In the spring of 2002, Ave Maria College had its first graduation. The seven graduating students, four young men and three young women, were all transfers from other institutions. Tom was particularly pleased that three of the four young men went on to seminary to study for the priesthood. Another pleasing aspect of this first graduation was Tom's satisfaction at being able to offer honorary degrees to Mother Angelica, foundress of EWTN, and Fr. Michael Scanlan, formerly president and at that time the chancellor of Franciscan University, whom Tom described as "two of my biggest heroes." Mother Angelica had recently suffered a stroke and was unable to travel to Ypsilanti to receive the award. This being so, Tom traveled with other representatives from AMC to her convent in Alabama to make the presentation and was amused at the way she tried to keep the academic cap on over her veil.

In the fall of 2002, there were around 180 students enrolled at the college, with a further hundred or so graduate students enrolled in the recently established Institute for Pastoral Theology. The law school had about 130 students, which was a little below Tom's hopes and expectations. There were sixty-five students in the incoming first-year class, slightly down from the seventy-six students who had enrolled in the inaugural class. That the law school was still going through the accreditation process may have impacted the number of enrollees.

Plans for the transition of the two campuses to Florida were proceeding apace. Nick Healy had already moved to Naples with his wife, Jane, so that he could pave the way for the rest of the AMU community to follow. Although Bernie Dobranski was less enthusiastic, reflecting the general air of skepticism prevailing at the law school, he agreed to the move south from the onset and vowed he would support it when it eventually came to a vote by the board.

Nonetheless, he convinced Tom to wait until the law school had successfully negotiated the accreditation process with the American Bar Association. Bishop Nevins, whose diocese of Venice included Naples, gave his blessing. "He couldn't have been more welcoming," Tom recalls. "He said it would be a privilege for the Diocese to have a Catholic University within its area."

In February of 2002, Tom visited Jim Coletta, the chairman of the Collier County Board of Commissioners, which oversaw development and construction in the area in which Tom hoped to build the new campus. "Jim was ecstatic," says Tom, desiring to do whatever was necessary to help Ave Maria proceed with its plans. "What a contrast to what I heard from the board of the Ann Arbor Township!" Tom then met the other four commissioners the following month, finding "each one enthusiastically supportive."

Having looked at a number of properties in the Naples area that were large enough for the proposed campus and having secured an option on one of them, Tom and Ave Maria University held a press conference at a local hotel to announce their plans to move the university to southwest Florida. "The interest was high. The room was packed. As a result of the media coverage, we received a call from Barron Collier Compan[ies], the largest landowner in the county." Originally, the Collier family had owned all of what is now Collier County, as well as swathes of land beyond it. They had 10,800 acres of land, about seventeen square miles, near Immokalee, about twenty miles inland from Naples, which they wished to develop. They offered to give the university the land it needed for its campus, completely free of charge, if the university would build it on their property. This was an offer that was too good to pass over. Contracts were signed and plans for construction were set in motion.

Tom had hoped that the cost of construction would be much lower in Florida because the construction industry is not unionized there, unlike in Michigan, and because there would be no issues with construction being halted due to seasonal problems, such as freezing in winter. He was wrong. "Our timing was terrible," he says. In 2004, as construction got under way, Florida experienced its worst hurricane season in living memory. Four major hurricanes struck southern Florida in August and September alone, with two more hitting the area in the following year. Although Florida was spared the deadly onslaught of Hurricane Katrina in 2005, the full impact of which fell on an unprepared New Orleans, the huge cleanup operation that followed in Katrina's wake created a major shortage of labor and materials. These weather-related obstacles to progress were exacerbated by the phenomenal rate of economic growth in southwest Florida, which was second only to Las Vegas, causing further shortages of labor and materials. The combined effect of these unforeseen factors doubled the projected costs of building the campus. "We couldn't afford to build all the buildings we planned," Tom lamented. "The big sacrifice was delaying the construction of the gym." Between the conception and the creation falls the shadow. . . .

During the period of construction, an interim campus was purchased in Naples for twenty-three million dollars.

It was compact, comprising two large three- and four-story midrise units, a clubhouse, and a dozen duplexes. In the fall of 2003, doors opened to new students, a little over a hundred in total, including many students who had chosen to transfer from the AMC campus in Michigan. In the previous November, the board of Ave Maria College had voted to essentially merge the college with the now officially formed Ave Maria University in Florida. Plans were made to close the campus in Ypsilanti, though the Ave Maria College Board agreed to keep the Michigan campus open until the summer of 2007. By the fall of the following year, the majority of students were at the Florida campus, which began the year with 337 students, more than three times as many as the previous year. By contrast, there were now only 119 students in Michigan, of which only twenty-nine were freshmen.

The exponential growth in Florida was creating the same problems for the university's interim campus in Naples as had the growth at the college's interim campus in Ypsilanti two years earlier. Although the Naples campus had been expanded, through the purchase of additional buildings in the vicinity, it was still ill-suited for the needs of a fast-expanding student body. "I don't know if we're going to make it by the fall of 2006," Nick Healy told *The Naples Daily News*, alluding to the date at which the new custom-built campus northeast of Naples was scheduled to be ready. "We're bursting at the seams," said Fr. Fessio, "but we'll find solutions."

Meanwhile, back in Michigan, the law school was not only flying high but flying highest in the whole state. Of those in the school's first graduating class (2003) who took the Michigan bar examination, an astonishing 93 percent passed. This pass rate was higher than any other law school in the state, an unprecedented achievement for a new law school, and a huge feather in Tom's cap. As if this were not exceptional enough, the graduating class of 2004 did even better, achieving an unsurpassable 100 percent passing rate.

The law school had 302 students in 2004, twenty-one faculty members, and a staff of almost fifty. "We did wonderful things in the first five years," Bernie Dobranski enthused. "We got ABA accreditation as fast as we could possibly get it. I never doubted that it would occur. The most important thing the ABA wanted to know was: Did we have solid financial resources? And the answer was: We had Tom Monaghan."

At this point, it appeared that Tom's investment of tens of millions of dollars was paying dividends and that the law school had indeed become the "first-class" Catholic institution of which he'd hoped, prayed, and dreamed. All was not well within its hallowed halls, however, as outraged members of its faculty, including some of the "Fired Five" whom Tom had hired when the school was founded, fought the move to Florida by tooth and nail and, eventually, lawsuit.

The anger, resentment, and dissent began to take its toll on the law school's performance. Although it once again did well in 2005, with its graduating class attaining a 96 percent passing rate for the Michigan bar examination, the third year in a row that it was the highest achieving law school in the state, the bubble was about to burst. "Students began transferring out in 2006–2007," said

Dobranski. "The dissident faculty members were encouraging students to transfer." Enrollment in that year was down to 331, compared with the high of 380 in the previous year. In truth, however, the fall in enrollment had at least as much to do with the significant decrease in tuition discounts or scholarships being offered to new students as it had to do with any negative impact that opposition to the move to Florida might have had. Tom was being forced to channel more of his resources than initially anticipated into the building of the new campus in Florida and therefore had little option but to reduce his financial input into the law school. It was in this sense, more than any other, that the transition to Florida could be said to be harming the law school, though Tom would no doubt have argued that it was a short-term sacrifice that would reap long-term benefits. Additionally, and to make matters worse, the law school was doing little in terms of fundraising and had missed its projected budgets.

On August 19, 2006, *The Wall Street Journal* published a balanced profile of Tom. It was entitled "Domino's Illuminatio Mea," a play on *Dominus illuminatio mea* (The Lord is my light), the opening words of the twenty-seventh psalm. The article began with Tom's oft-expressed desire "to get as many people into heaven as possible." This at least provided the correct perspective and proper focus for any discussion of Tom's motives, even if, inevitably and predictably, the article discussed the shadow that had fallen on his best-laid schemes because of the "vitriolic battle" between the pro-Florida and anti-Florida factions at the law school. The article ended on an upbeat note, quoting

Tom's self-effacing assertion that he relied on the intelligence and wisdom of the team with which he surrounded himself. "I've always believed in hiring people smarter than I am," he told *The Wall Street Journal*'s reporter. "I should be the dumbest person in the room." Clearly impressed by the man she'd interviewed, the reporter ended her profile with a gentle rebuttal of these words. Begging to differ with Tom's humble assessment of himself, she concluded with the simple assertion that, whatever else he might be, Tom Monaghan was emphatically *not* the dumbest person in the room.

Irrespective of the ongoing discussion in the media, and in spite of the entrenched opposition of a significant portion of the faculty, the board of Ave Maria School of Law voted on February 17, 2007, to move the law school to Florida. Three days later, Bernie Dobranski made the decision public in a press release. At this time, the new campus, surrounded by the embryonic town of Ave Maria, was on the verge of opening. The university, which now had almost five hundred students, had been crammed into the interim campus in Naples for four years and was in dire need of more spacious facilities. It was, therefore, with great relief that the university officially moved into its new home, twenty miles away, at the beginning of the fall semester in 2007, a year later than originally planned.

CHAPTER 18

A LIGHT BREAKS

NOT SURPRISINGLY, the long-awaited opening of the new custom-built campus created a lot of media interest. *GQ*, in an article entitled "Hail Mary USA," observed something curious about the very orientation of the newly constructed town surrounding the campus: "The street grid of Ave Maria, Florida, is skewed precisely 2.49 degrees north of east so that the . . . eastern avenues will catch the sunrise each March 25, the day on which Catholics traditionally mark the feast of the Annunciation." In point of fact, if the streets were oriented in that manner, they were merely conforming to the orientation of the newly opened oratory, which, apart from its dominating the skyline, had been oriented so that the first rays of the sun on the feast of the Annunciation would shine through the window and fall on the altar of the church. In an example of the suggestiveness that characterized his biography of Tom, James Leonard implied on two separate occasions that this orientation was Tom's egotistical idea to celebrate his own birthday, which happens to coincide with the feast day. Thus, in quoting the above passage from

GQ, Leonard observes that the author of the article "failed to mention that March 25 is also Tom Monaghan's birthday" (292).

Why, one wonders, did Leonard not simply ask Tom directly whether the orientation of the Oratory had been his idea and, if so, whether it had anything to do with his birthday? Had he done so, he would have discovered that Tom had nothing to do with this decision, which was the brainchild of Fr. Fessio. The present author recalls discussions with Fr. Fessio at the time of the Oratory's construction in which he waxed with great enthusiasm about this Christocentric aspect of the Oratory's design, which he had persuaded everyone to accept.

Doing what Leonard should have done, I asked Tom directly about Leonard's suggestion that the Oratory's orientation was an ego trip on his part, designed as a birthday present to himself. Tom told me what I already knew, that he had nothing to do with the decision and that the whole thing was Fr. Fessio's idea.

As light was breaking on the new campus, and the new town of Ave Maria that was growing up around it, the sun was setting on Tom's increasingly tempestuous working relationship with Fr. Fessio. In July 2009, Fr. Fessio was unceremoniously fired from his position at AMU. I was with him at the moment he received the news and was with him for the remainder of the day. I was also present when he made phone calls to his Jesuit superior in California to tell him of the news. We were driving together to Tampa for a Catholic homeschooling conference, at which we were both speaking, and we stayed in the same hotel.

As such, I have a better firsthand memory of what happened on that day than almost anyone except for Jack Sites, AMU's vice-president for academic affairs, who did the firing, and Fr. Fessio himself. I say this to establish my own bona fide credentials and to thereby dissipate the fog that characterizes Leonard's discussion of this episode. I would add, by way of full disclosure, that I considered Fr. Fessio one of my closest friends and still do.

Fr. Fessio's dismissal from any role at AMU came as no real surprise to him or to anyone else. His relationship with Tom and particularly with Nick Healy, AMU's president, had become increasingly strained. Indeed, he had already been fired once before, three years earlier, but the opposition of the student body, who demonstrated publicly in his support on the interim campus, and phone calls from outraged donors led to his reinstatement the following day. He was, however, not reinstated as provost, the authoritative position he had held at the time of his first firing, having previously been chancellor, but only to the effectively powerless position of theologian-in-residence.

The reason for Fr. Fessio's initial dismissal was because he and Nick Healy were at such loggerheads that they were no longer able to work together.

The enmity arose largely from their differences over the way that the liturgy should be celebrated on campus. Fr. Fessio was very tradition-oriented and adhered to the liturgical teaching in Cardinal Ratzinger's book, *The Spirit of the Liturgy*, whereas Healy favored the sort of charismatic "praise and worship" liturgies that had been the norm at Franciscan University when Nick had been there.

I know from my own discussions with him that Fr. Fessio was angered by what he perceived as Nick's unwarranted interference in the way that the liturgy was celebrated.

Another factor, equally and perhaps even more important than the liturgical differences, was that Fr. Fessio was becoming increasingly skeptical of the direction in which Tom and Nick were taking the university. He thought that the strategy of fast-track growth, in terms of student numbers and the number of majors being offered, was compromising the spiritual and academic quality of the student body, and that the decision to add a large number of sports programs would further erode AMU's spiritual identity. He and I collaborated on a "vision unfolding" document in which we sought to dissuade Tom and Nick from going gung ho into sports and to try to find ways to increase the size of the student body more slowly in order to ensure that spiritual and academic standards were maintained.

In short, Fr. Fessio's vision for the university was diverging from that which Tom and Nick were pursuing, and his strained and estranged relationship with Nick was such that the two men could no longer effectively work together. This was the reason for Fr. Fessio being fired the first time. Following his reinstatement to the faculty as theologian-in-residence, he had no real power to influence the direction the university was taking but remained perhaps a thorn in the side of the powers that be. His being fired the second time was a consequence of his circulation of details of the university's finances to certain members of the board, an act that he would justify as a necessary intervention on his part for the good of the university but that was considered by the overall board of trustees to be a breach of trust that could have harmful effects on the university's development.

What is perhaps remarkable, and consoling, is the way that Tom has apparently not harbored any grudge or bitterness against Fr. Fessio in spite of their parting on such unfortunate terms. "I traveled with him a lot," he remembers. "I had some of my happiest times with him and some of my most miserable. He can be the greatest friend and is such a likeable person." What was also exemplary was the way that Tom fielded questions from James Leonard, who was clearly looking to have some scandal to report. Far from seeking to blame Fr. Fessio for the way things turned out, Tom was at pains to praise him. "He's very bright. He's orthodox, passionate." But why, Leonard persisted, was there so much confusion over Fr. Fessio's role when he came to AMU? "We probably did him a misjustice [sic]," Tom responded. "The whole idea was to get him out of that situation he was in: one of the best-known priests in the country, and he was put into exile. I don't think we thought out what the role would be. I failed. I didn't find a way to have him fit in with the organization. It would've taken some doing, but I probably could've found a way to do it."

Leonard asked Tom again about his former friend, implying that Fr. Fessio was telling everyone his side of the story with regard to the reasons for his being fired. Again, Tom's response was the height of charitable decorum: "He didn't like the way things were being run, he was courageous enough to say it, and for saying it, for his courage, he got fired. Leave it at that." Leonard would not leave it at that. He tried again. Was it true that he felt that Fr. Fessio had betrayed his trust? Was that why he was fired? After a brief pause, Tom responded: "Fr. Fessio. . . . He's a great gift to the Church. Ignatius Press has done great things for the Church. I'm surprised somebody at one of these smaller Catholic schools hasn't tried to hire him. I think it'd be a good move on their part" (317–18).

At this point, Leonard was forced to admit that "[i]t was clear Monaghan really did wish Fessio well." In fact, had he been more astute, he would have detected in Tom's final response, a clue to why the two friends had to part. When all was said and done, and when the dust had settled, Tom's idea of what Ave Maria University needed to become was very different from Fr. Fessio's. In Tom's view, not only did Ave Maria need to grow into something that was much bigger than the sort of small Catholic school, such as Christendom College, at which he felt Fr. Fessio would be more comfortable, but it was on a trajectory to even outgrow larger Catholic schools, such as Franciscan University, from which AMU received its original inspiration. Unlike Franciscan University, which had decided against building a law school and was not interested in grandiose sports programs, Ave Maria University would forge forward as a new Notre Dame, though one that would not renege on its Catholic mission and identity.

The problems associated with the firing of Fr. Fessio were as nothing compared to those associated with the law school. The rebellion having effectively been crushed, the law school moved to Florida in 2009 with only a handful of the original faculty still on board. Due to the escalating construction costs at the new campus, the site planned for the law school on the AMU campus had not even begun to be built. Instead the law school moved into what had been AMU's interim campus, known as the Vineyards Campus, which had been vacated two years earlier by the university. The problems that the rebellion had caused, not least of which was a lawsuit brought by three former faculty members, was spelled out in a headline in *The Naples Daily News* earlier in the year: "Ave Maria Law School Spends More than $1 Million in Legal Fees Last Year." Inevitably, such headlines harmed the law school's reputation. The 2009 *U.S. News & World Report* law school rankings placed Ave Maria as tied for last place in the peer-assessment category. In addition, the US Department of Education reported that the law school had failed its financial responsibility test, the only law school in the country to have done so. It was all a long way from the halcyon days of its founding, when it had flown high above its long-established and venerable rivals in terms of achievement.

Reflecting on the bitterness of the rebellion at the college and law school, Tom seems to lick his wounds, and then, as he's done repeatedly in the past as the owner of Domino's, he seems to bounce back from the crisis with an irrepressible optimism. "It's difficult to believe what we've been through. You know, it was incredible how we managed to fix all the drama that was there in Michigan." He pauses, as if pondering the past and the scars that he and others, on both sides, bore from its travails. "It was bizarre. How I had the ability to just keep going and not be bitter about it, I'll never know."

Yet he did keep going and things began to improve dramatically, especially at the law school. Bernie Dobranski had stepped down due to a chronic health issue and Gene Milhizer had taken over as Dean. By 2010, after only one year at the new campus in Naples, Milhizer waxed with eloquence and enthusiasm about the progress made in the previous twelve months. In spite of the move from one state to another, the law school had kept its ABA accreditation, the loss of which might have been truly disastrous. "We kept our full accreditation because we satisfied the key criteria," Milhizer enthused. The ABA team that had traveled to Florida to appraise the school for accreditation purposes reported that "they'd never seen an institution where everybody has as deep a commitment to and understanding of the mission as at our law school, that they'd never seen a school with better esprit de corps than ours. No one would have said that a few years earlier."

It was indeed a truly remarkable turnaround. The incoming class in 2010 was the largest ever, LSAT scores had improved, and the number of self-identified Catholics in the student body had increased. "So," Milhizer said, with evident satisfaction, "we have achieved all our goals." After such a dark shadow had fallen over the fortunes of the law school, it seemed that the light was finally beginning to break through. This was evident in Milhizer's assessment of Ave Maria School of Law's importance in the culture wars. "Our society is run by lawyers, for better or worse, and I think that there is a real place at the table for a school that says not everything is relative, that some things are evil and some things are really good, and that words have meaning.

When you see this played out in the real world, there are real consequences. The culture will be a better culture when our graduates start assuming positions of authority." Tom could not have put it better himself, and one could see why Dean Milhizer was a man after Tom's own heart.

Having completed the law school's move to Florida and overseen its firm establishment in both the greater Naples community and southwest Florida, Gene Milhizer longed to return to the classroom. After performing a national search, the law school board hired Kevin Cieply to be the third president and dean, a post he assumed on July 1, 2014. Cieply, a retired US Army colonel and former Judge Advocate General Corps (JAG) officer and helicopter pilot, had most recently served as the associate dean of academics and associate professor at Atlanta's John Marshall Law School. While things were settled in terms of the past unrest related to the move from Michigan to Florida, Cieply took the helm at a time when law school enrollment across the country was down, thus a very competitive environment for student recruitment.

Cieply was totally on board with the law school's mission, "We know what our purpose is," he explained. "We aren't struggling to find our niche or our relevance. We know we've got a clearly defined mission . . . to make Catholic education relevant and a change agent for society." And the law school is gaining recognition for this niche. In the spring of 2016, for the second time, it was named the best Catholic law school in the United States for the devout by the National Jurist's *PreLaw Magazine*. An inkling of what a difference might be made by the new generation of lawyers graduating from the AMSL could be gleaned from the great work being done by the Thomas More Law Center to preserve religious freedom in the wake of the Obama administrations attacks upon it. The TMLC, which was funded in its early years with Tom's seed money and subsidies, was coming of age in its crusade against iniquitous law, as exemplified in its bringing of a lawsuit in 2010 against US Attorney General Eric Holder, challenging the constitutionality of the recently enacted Hate Crimes Act, which criminalizes the calling of homosexual acts sinful. The TMLC was forthright in its condemnation of the draconian nature of such a law, insisting in its press release that its "sole purpose . . . is to criminalize the Bible, and to use the threat of federal prosecution and long jail sentences to silence Christians."

Even bolder was the Thomas More Law Center's courageous stand against Obamacare. Within minutes of the passage of the Affordable Care Act, also in 2010, the TMLC had filed a lawsuit against President Obama and Secretary of Health and Human Services Kathleen Sebelius, along with Attorney General Eric Holder and Secretary of the Treasury Timothy Geithner. Once again, the TMLC's language in its press release was forthright and uncompromising: "This Act is a product of political corruption and the exercise of unconstitutional power. Our Founding Fathers envisioned a limited form of government. The purpose of our Constitution and this lawsuit is to insure it stays that way." Anyone who values traditional liberties and fears the encroachment of ever larger and intrusive government will feel heartened by fighting talk such as this, buttressed as it is by the force of law, and will be thankful not only for the work of the TMLC but for the funding of Tom Monaghan, without which the TMLC would never have gotten off the ground.

If the Thomas More Law Center could be said to be coming of age in 2010, the same could be said of Legatus, which continued to grow and prosper. In 2010, four new chapters were founded, in Colorado Springs, Pittsburgh, Napa Valley, and Hollywood (an outpost in the heart of the beast!). In April 2011, the tenth Legatus Pro-Life Conference was held in Washington DC, and in the same year, two new chapters were founded in California and another in Lexington, Kentucky. Then, in February 2012, Legatus celebrated the twenty-fifth anniversary of its founding at its annual summit in Naples, Florida. After continued growth, Legatus had over two thousand CEOs and their spouses as members. Three years later, this had risen to over 2,500 members in more than eighty chapters across the length and breadth of the United States, a vast array of successful business leaders being strengthened in their Faith to do the work of the Church and engaging the broader culture. In July 2016, Stephen Henley, an Ave Maria University graduate, became the sixth executive director of Legatus.

There were also signs that things were looking brighter for the university. The Southern Association of Colleges and Schools (SACS) finally granted AMU full accreditation in 2010, after years of seemingly interminable delay, and the Oratory, towering like a guardian of faith over the campus, was finally consecrated. After years of struggle in which, at times, the storm clouds had descended to cast dark and ominous shadows, it looked as though the sun was finally breaking through. And yet, just when it seemed that a period of calm was approaching, Tom decided that, in February 2011, he would relinquish the reins at AMU to make way for his successor, Jim Towey, to take over as both president and CEO. Towey was chosen by the board to serve after a national search. He had been president of St. Vincent College in Pennsylvania from 2006 to 2010, and prior to that, he served under President George W. Bush as the director of the White House's Office of Faith-Based and Community Initiatives. Although Tom would retain the title of chancellor at the request of the board, it was a purely honorary position without any administrative authority over the future direction of the school. He did, however, stay on as a member of the board of trustees. For James Leonard, never one to offer praise lightly (or usually at all), Tom's stepping down was "more than amazing: it was an incredible act of self-denial" (374). For those who knew Tom better, his stepping aside was less of a surprise. He had walked away from Domino's to pursue his spiritual goals, leaving behind a global empire that he had built and rebuilt. Why would he not be able to walk away from the day-to-day operations of the university he'd founded when he felt the time was ripe and right? He was seventy-four years old and ready to step aside, allowing the weight of responsibility to fall on Towey's younger shoulders. He was not, however, ready to hang up his boots and retire.

CHAPTER 19

LIFE ON THE SIDELINES

ONCE TOM had accepted his new backseat role at Ave Maria University, he had no desire to be a backseat driver. On the contrary, and embracing his honorary role as the university's chancellor with alacrity, he was more than happy for Towey to take the wheel. And yet, and to stay with the metaphor, his money was still needed to put gas in the tank. During the 2011–2012 academic year, his contribution to AMU was approximately seven million dollars, and his underwriting of the cost of the town of Ave Maria amounted to another five million. Over the next couple of years, Tom's subsidy of the university would lessen each year to the point of AMU's self-sufficiency by 2014. In terms of the town, while it has decreased over time due to the town's growth, his subsidy is expected to be needed until the end of 2017. In contrast, most of the other entities that he had founded or supported as part of what might be called his post-Domino's spiritual empire were then independent of his money and continued to operate on their own. These included the Ave Maria School of Law; the Thomas More Law Center; the Dominican Sisters of Mary, Mother of the Eucharist; Ave Maria Radio; Ave Maria Singles; and Legatus.

Considering the constant drain that the university and town of Ave Maria have been on his resources it is not surprising that he looks at the whole project with an air of wistfulness. When I asked him whether he thought that his fifty-fifty partnership with the Barron Collier Companies to build the town was a marriage made in heaven, he responded that he thought, in hindsight, that it may have been a mistake.

I was surprised. A mistake?

"I'm not sure," he responded, perhaps backtracking slightly. "So far, the finances have not worked out as I had hoped."

Why would he say that?

"Because the timing was so bad for developing a housing project." Tom went on to clarify, "Don't get me wrong, it was a good idea, and the Colliers are great partners; it has just tied up so much money over such a long period of time. I always envisioned our share of the profits from the development of the town creating a significant endowment for the university; this financial strength would enable the university to accomplish even greater things as it grows." Since this conversation with Tom, the town of Ave Maria has continued to build momentum and has been one of the fifty fastest-growing communities in the country for the past two years, and the outlook is very positive. Sales for the first half of 2016 were at a record pace, surpassing the two previous record years.

It is true that the project coincided with the catastrophic collapse in the property market throughout the United States, and in Florida especially, but could Tom have been realistically expected to have known about the radical downturn in the market? And, if he couldn't, could the partnership with Barron Collier really be called a mistake? Although, with the wisdom of *hindsight*, it might appear to have been a mistake, might the partnership, made as it was without the wisdom of *foresight*, best be considered a misfortune rather than a mistake? Tom was only partially mollified by such a suggestion:

> Perhaps I shouldn't have done it. I've put maybe $150 million in that whole venture. If I had put that money in an Ave Maria Mutual Fund, the investment would probably be worth $250 million today. I think of all those years and all the grief which came with them, and all the sacrifices I made, both personally and financially . . . I essentially commuted between Florida and Michigan on a weekly basis, which took its toll. Also, because of financial reasons, we made sacrifices, and all the years I had to walk on financial thin ice and couldn't do a lot of things I wanted to for the university; that really was hard. I was selling everything I could find to try to keep pulling another rabbit out of the hat and keep it going. It was tough financially.

Regardless of such regrets and concerns, Tom remains confident about the university's future. The property market is looking more buoyant, more homes are being built

in Ave Maria, and as of June 30, 2015, the university is no
longer dependent financially on Tom. In the fall of 2014,
AMU's enrollment exceeded one thousand students for the
first time, and in the fall of 2016, it is offering thirty-three
undergraduate majors plus its master's and doctorate programs. Furthermore, in December 2015, the university was
reaccredited by SACS for another ten years.

Tom's own confidence and ongoing commitment are
demonstrated in his granting of scholarships to students
from his own native Michigan to attend AMU. He hosts
many events in Ann Arbor for prospective students and
has a year-long recruiting effort, which includes a fly-in
effort that sends high school seniors to AMU for a weekend college visit. He also puts on an annual dinner dance
to raise scholarship funds, doing his best to continue to
help the university he founded from the sidelines and
remembering also, perhaps, the days when his own plans
for a university education had been curtailed by a lack of
funds. He is certainly proud of the fact that year after year
the university is listed in the Cardinal Newman Guide
(first published in 2007), which recommends twenty US
Catholic colleges and universities for their faithful Catholic
identity. "Helping our students get to heaven has to be our
top priority, or we are missing the whole point," Tom says.
When he founded AMU, the Catholic mission was at the
center of the university's identity, and Tom believes that
this continues to be the case—not only in the classroom
but throughout campus. Students have the opportunity to
avail themselves of Mass, offered three times a day in the
Oratory, and there is perpetual Eucharistic adoration on

campus, a nightly, student-led rosary walk, more than sixty student run clubs and organizations, and many service projects. Tom muses, "When I see these young students on fire with their faith, I am excited about the impact they will have on our country and the Church."

Although one could never imagine Tom living life in the slow lane, life on the sidelines has its consolations and advantages, not least of which is that he now has more time to spend with Margie and their children and grandchildren. He also has more time to indulge his passion for music. He had first learned to play the E-flat alto horn as a child in the orphanage but gave up playing music as an adult until he came across a horn in an antique shop sometime in the 1990s. He now plays the trumpet as well as the alto horn but, by his own estimation, is "not very good at either of them." He enjoys playing classic songs from the golden age of songwriting, such as "I Left My Heart in San Francisco," but his favorite song, and the one he enjoys playing most on his alto horn or trumpet, is Hoagy Carmichael's "Stardust." He asked me if I knew it, to which I replied that I did but could not quite remember the tune. He then surprised me by breaking into song:

> Sometimes I wonder why I spend
> The lonely night dreaming of a song.
> The melody haunts my reverie,
> And I am once again with you
> When our love was new
> And each kiss an inspiration,
> But that was long ago.

Now my consolation
Is in the stardust of a song.

Having surprised me with his vocal rendition, he then
waxed lyrical about the song itself, telling me that "sometime in the 1960s, it was declared the most popular song of
all time." It had been recorded by more than two thousand
artists, he informed me. "Bing Crosby was the first to have
a hit with it, and Nat King Cole the last."

I realized—somewhat to my surprise, I must confess—
that I had inadvertently tapped into a real passion of
Tom's that is unknown to all but his most intimate circle of
friends. I was keen to know more.

"Well, I like music," he explained. "The music I like,
I like. I don't like rock. I was a big, big Bing Crosby fan.
And I was an Al Jolson fan. And a lot of girls liked Al Jolson when I was younger, you know. In fact, I think sometime in the forties he was number one for record sales in
the country." I asked him whether he wasn't a bit young to
be a fan of Bing Crosby and Al Jolson. Weren't young men
of his generation, growing up in the fifties, more likely to
like rock 'n' roll? He conceded the point, at least up to a
point, admitting that he was only in the ninth grade when
Al Jolson died in 1950, but he added that he had grown
up with Bing Crosby. "We were fed Bing Crosby in the
orphanage." He used to imitate Jolson. "I think I used to
be pretty good, at least in the shower!" He also liked Bobby
Darin ("He takes an old standard and gives it this incredible personality") but is less enthusiastic about Frank Sinatra. "I can live with Frank Sinatra, although I don't think

he was as great as a lot of people think. You listen to Bing and Frank Sinatra side by side, between the voice and the style, and there's only one winner." He laments, however, that people forget how good Bing Crosby actually was because, by the time he was seen regularly on television, his great voice was in decline.

Personally, as one who had only really experienced Tom Monaghan as a somewhat aloof figure, a little socially awkward perhaps, it was a real revelation to see him come to life when talking about music. This was brought home even more vividly when Ed Pear, Tom's lawyer and probably his closest friend, described the great times that he and Tom have had at the annual conventions of the Al Jolson Society. "Tom can be . . . just a lot of fun. He's in the Al Jolson Society, and once a year they have their convention. I don't think many people could picture Tom Monaghan in a bar at ten or eleven at night where all fifty or so people that were there were singing Jolson songs, just standing over by the piano singing, and Tom's singing all the songs with all the rest of them and having a good time." Ed Pear's vision of Tom's seldom seen joie de vivre and rambunctious abandon was corroborated by Tom himself: "This weekend in Orlando I am going to the annual Al Jolson Festival. I am a big-time fan. Everybody talks about Al Jolson, and they have an Al Jolson impersonator, and we go to the bar afterward, and a lot of people stay up, and we sing Al Jolson songs until the wee hours. I absolutely love it. I am taking the same group as most years—my attorney, Ed Pear, Judge Conlin, and our wives."

Ed Pear and Tom, and their respective wives, often go on vacations together, visiting art museums and architectural landmarks, or just hanging out at the Monaghans' house in Florida, and Pear recalls, with a chuckle, that Tom always takes his horn with him, playing it in the morning. "He always has to play 'Margie,'" says Pear. "That's his favorite song." Notwithstanding the fact that Tom would no doubt beg to differ with his friend, having declared "Stardust" to be his favorite, "Margie" is nonetheless a song that means a lot to Tom personally and was the first tune he taught himself to play on the horn when he took it up again in the nineties. A song made famous by Eddie Cantor in the twenties and recorded by many others, including Al Jolson and Bing Crosby, Tom's own partiality for the song is obviously linked to the fact that Margie is the name of his own beloved wife.

His love for Margie is unabated, the abiding love of his life, rising above all other passions except for his love of God. He is also very family oriented, his eyes lighting up when I ask him to identify a photograph in his office. "Oh, that's my granddaughter," he beamed. "She's five foot one, and she's a first-team All-State soccer player, two years in a row. She's now playing at Hope College, and she scored the winning goal in the championship game as a freshman in a shootout." At the time of writing, Tom had ten grandchildren—seven boys and three girls—and two great-grandchildren. "Grandkids are really special," he says. "The best reason to have kids is because they have kids!" He enjoys playing with them and feels blessed that they live nearby, in homes that he had built especially for two of his daughters. "I built a compound to lure them," he explains, "to lure my daughters to live near us." The houses are two hundred or three hundred feet apart, one on each side of his and Margie's own house, and wooded so that the three houses are not visible from each other. He built an elaborate tree house on the property, which the grandchildren enjoy, and had a playroom built in his own house to make the grandparents' a fun place to visit. "They come over all the time. We have a lot of fun times."

When the oldest of his grandsons was only five years old, Tom teamed up with him to build a large, grandiose shack, which they called the Tar Paper Shack, designing it together. "That was really fun, taking him around to flea markets and junkyards," Tom remembers. "A five-year-old kid who is so curious and hangs on every word that I say."

Margie is as doting in her relationship with their grandchildren as is Tom. "My wife is a great grandmother," Tom says. "She just loves those grandkids and they love her. It's unconditional love."

Margie is "big on Christmas," he says, and she even owns her very own Christmas store. "She decorates the house to the hilt and does all the cooking herself and all the cleaning up. And she has a wrapping room that would put any department store wrapping room to shame. And the rolls of wrapping paper and ribbons! You've seen nothing like it!" Every Christmas, the whole family spends the day together, the four daughters, their husbands, the ten grandchildren, and the great-grandchildren.

Easter and Thanksgiving are also huge family gatherings, with the whole clan gathering for a huge feast that

Margie cooks herself. "Margie will be in the kitchen for days, cooking up a storm. She is good at it. It is a production—she'll have a million different things going at once." On lesser holidays—such as Memorial Day, the Fourth of July, and Labor Day—Margie will do barbecues, gathering the whole family under her maternal wings like a mother hen. On Sundays, she and Tom attend St. Thomas's in downtown Ann Arbor, the church in which they were married, and afterward, when they get home, they have caterers bring in food, "and the kids sort of drop in over the course of the day, which is kind of nice."

Although Tom is no longer able to exercise as vigorously as in his younger days, physical fitness is still a major priority. There is no more running of marathons or running six miles a day, but he still tries to walk for about an hour every morning. And he's still in great shape, working out with weights.

Spiritual fitness is also a priority. He rises every day at 3 a.m. and begins the day with an hour of adoration before the Blessed Sacrament at the nearby church of Christ the King. Then, after a light breakfast of fruit, he does his daily physical workout. Five mornings a week, he does aerobics, followed by a walk, and on the remaining two mornings, he works out with weights for two hours. "With aerobics I do two 40 minute sessions on the Stairmaster, and I get my pulse up to 135; that's my goal, and I make sure I do it each time. Sometimes it's pretty tough. And then I might do a little elliptical and a little treadmill with the thing way up so I can get my pulse up. And then I walk. I do a little stretching maybe." He has just enough time after his workout and walk to shower and freshen up before Mass at 8 a.m.

After Mass and morning prayer he has a second break-fast, usually an omelet. I quipped at this point that he must be a hobbit because hobbits always have a second break-fast. He looked puzzled. I asked him whether he had ever read *The Hobbit* or *The Lord of the Rings*. He told me that he had tried to read it after he had heard me give a talk at Ave Maria University on the Catholicism of *The Lord of the Rings* but that he couldn't get through all the strange names of the characters and places in Tolkien's world.

At around 9 a.m., he does some work in his office, and then, at around 10 a.m., he takes a well-earned rest, nap-ping on a reclining chair in his office for about an hour and a half. After a lunch, which usually consists solely of soup, he has appointments in the afternoon, followed by evening prayer at 4:45. Somewhere in the midst of this already busy schedule, often during his workouts or his daily walk, he says at least one Rosary a day, a prayer routine that puts most of us to shame. The evenings are reserved for family and friends. On two or three evenings, he and Margie will go out to dinner with friends, and the rest of the week, they spend at home or visiting with their children and grand-children in the neighboring houses.

Surveying a typical day in the life of Tom Monaghan as he approaches his eightieth birthday, one is struck by how well balanced it is and how well balanced he seems to be. As he keeps in graceful equilibrium the demands and responsibilities of faith and family, and of physical and spiritual fitness, it would appear that Tom is truly enjoying his life on the sidelines.

CHAPTER 20

SEMPER FIDELIS

Semper Fidelis
Always Faithful

Motto of the US Marine Corps

IT WOULD be easy and tempting, now that he is in his sunset years, for Tom to sit back with a degree of satisfaction over the life he's lived and to rest on his laurels. He is, however, on his guard against the temptation of smugness or arrogance.

> I think I have always had a stronger-than-average urge to impress people. I don't know where that came from. I think that was probably my upbringing, where I was always sort of poor, embarrassed about the situation that I was in, not having the things that other kids had, particularly a normal family. I think that was the thing that I was most embarrassed about. I always resented the fact that I had to have bad luck that my dad died. I was always thinking *"Why did that have to happen?"* I always had

239

this feeling that when I grow up it's going to be different, and I'll be in charge and do what I want to do and not be restricted.

Now, having been so successful, I would say that I have to be careful because so many people applaud me and compliment me that I have to make sure that I am doing things for the greater glory of God and not for self. I try to pray a lot about being humble, because I guess I have been in the position for a long time of being arrogant and having my way and having people catering to me. I have to pray a lot. I try to remember that my job, my main job, is to become a saint. It's not something that I think about often enough but that is my main job. I need to treat people as if they are the most important people, giving and being charitable and resisting my selfish tendencies. We are born to praise God, and that is why it feels good and when we do it we feel better. It's a joy. It might not be happiness as the world knows it, but it's deeper.

Seeing life with a serenity born of experience, he has made peace with himself and with his past, even those parts of it that were most painful. I asked him, for instance, whether there were still dark recesses of his mind and heart in which he still resented his mother's neglect of him as a child. "No," he replied. "I don't think so, no. She always wanted to do the right thing; she just sometimes didn't know how. People used to often tell me, a lot of my relatives would tell me, how unfair my mother was to me, but I would say that she was a good mom. I always defended her." It was evident that he had forgiven his mother and was trying to forget the bad times, preferring to linger on the happier memories. "I'll tell you, she was a walking encyclopedia. Just so much memory. A lot of things I know today I learned from the short time I was with her."

In similar fashion, he looks back on his time in the Marine Corps with fondness, showing great respect for its formative influence on his own life, almost as if the Marines had been a surrogate father to him.

> I have a lot of good feelings for the Marine Corps. I think I owe a lot of what I have done to the Corps. I think they pushed me further than I ever thought I could be pushed, and I survived it. I hated it externally when I was in. I couldn't wait until the day that I got out—but down deep I thought that it was something that I was sure glad that I was going through. There is something special about the Marine Corps, though I don't know if it is the same today as it was then. It was hell. They are experts at harassment, and it's a great character builder. A lot of people don't make it. They are cut loose before they get through the twelve weeks of boot camp. It gave me a lot of confidence. I felt that if I can deal with this, I can deal with anything. I liked the physical part of it. It was kind of a family, too. You know, it was like the first family I had. They say it's the largest fraternity in the world.

Even into old age, Tom was associating himself with other USMC veterans, being involved with the Marine Corps League, and commemorating the Marine Corps birthday on November 10. "Every marine knows the Marine Corps birthday," he says.

Although there is little doubt that Tom has lived up to the USMC motto to be "always faithful" (*semper fidelis*), his fidelity to the Marines is tempered by its place in a greater hierarchy of faithfulness. At the top of this hierarchy is, of course, Tom's sense of duty to God and His Church. He feels, in this area, that he has not always lived up to his responsibility to serve as an appropriate role model:

> I didn't pull off the role model thing very well. As a successful Catholic in the financial world, I had the idea that I was meant to be a role model, but there were a lot of mess-ups along the way. I really blew it. I had this compulsion for all these luxuries, and I was so foolish and so stupid, especially when I think of what I could have done. But it was so obvious to me after I read Lewis's *Mere Christianity* that I was exactly the kind of person I hated: a show-off. Thank God I had a second chance.

In retrospect, however, he is not completely happy with the way that he handled his "second chance." He had been deeply impacted by his work with Fr. Enrique in poverty-stricken Honduras in the 1980s and wishes that he had spent more of his wealth on the needs of the world's poor. "If I were doing it all over again," he muses. "I would consider spending much more of my money in the third world." Almost wistfully, he imagines how many seminaries and convents he could have helped build in the developing world for the money he had spent on so many other projects.

Back in 1986, on one of his visits to Central America, Tom had been greatly affected by the experience of attending Mass in Fr. Enrique's makeshift parish church. "I wasn't quite prepared for the emotional impact the service would have on me," he said. Witnessing the faith of the children of the parish, he was overwhelmed by the experience of seeing "the ragged children who filled the rough-hewn benches that served as pews," adding that he hadn't felt "that kind of spiritual identification with a group of youngsters since I left the orphanage." A similar emotional experience awaited him much more recently, in 2013, when he visited some orphanages in Mexico run by an order of sisters established by Fr. Aloysius Schwartz, a missionary priest who worked in Korea and the Philippines, as well as in Mexico. (In 2015 Fr. Schwartz was decreed to be Venerable by Pope Francis, a step toward what might eventually be his canonization.) He explains,

> I went to one orphanage, which had three thousand girls from about twelve to eighteen years old. All their uniforms they made themselves. They have a trade school for them. They'd all learn a trade. And every single one of those girls gets a job when they finish their high school. They were all well-formed in the faith. We went to this huge gym, probably eight courts, and they all have this little plastic stool.

They're sitting on that stool for Mass, and they're sitting straight, perfect attention; no talking, no snick-
ering back and forth. They had a music program that
you wouldn't believe; I cried like a baby.

One can imagine, as with the earlier experience with
the poor children in Honduras, that Tom's own childhood
years in an orphanage enabled him to empathize and sympathize deeply with these girls, reducing him to tears as
he felt a deep-seated affinity with these outcasts from traditional family life. One can also see why he might wish
that he'd spent more of his considerable fortune on girls
and boys such as these rather than on the comparatively
well-off students who are benefitting from the schools
he'd helped to establish in the United States. "The truth
is," he says, "I've done a fraction of what I could and should
have done."

Putting such regrets aside, Tom Monaghan is contented with his own relative poverty and does not miss the
huge wealth he'd possessed in the past nor its glamorous
trappings. "I don't feel bad about it," he says. "I'd like to
have more money, I'd like to be younger, but I feel pretty
satisfied with my situation. I have everything I need. I don't
have any yearning for any kind of luxuries." He has his
faith and he has his family and, more to the point, he is
resolved to be always faithful to both. What else could he
or should he want?

CHAPTER 21

LOOKING AT THE STARS

BACK IN 2011, in a particularly candid interview with James Leonard, Tom spoke about his relationship with God, saying that he was "trying to live in the presence of God all the time": "I say a prayer before I get a phone call or a meeting. . . . I don't do it all the time. I do it when I think of it. I should do it more. My goal is to constantly live within the presence of God, to be aware of the presence of God. I should be constantly aware of the one who created me and sustains me."

Leonard was incredulous, asking him whether it was possible to do this and still live a life at the same time. Tom's response was both eloquent and profound: "Nobody does it perfectly. One thing that all the saints have in common is that they're heavily aware of their weaknesses, their sins of omission, of not giving God enough credit, thanking him enough, praising him enough. The greatest saints seem to be more aware of what's really important in life: serving God and loving God and accepting his love and giving that love to everyone else because the way you treat others is the way you treat God" (385).

The extent to which Tom was trying to practice what he preached was evident in Leonard's admission that Tom answered all his questions "as frankly and honestly as he could, though he wouldn't speak ill of the living and only very rarely of the dead."

For Leonard, a nonbeliever who does not conceal his hostility to Catholicism, such a way of living one's life was decidedly odd. "However you define the word and whether or not he'd admit it; Monaghan was eccentric."

In an effort to see whether Tom would admit to being an eccentric, Leonard asked him outright and confessed to being "surprised" by Tom's answer: "I hope I do come off as eccentric . . . because a lot of people will feel that someone who's a traditional Catholic might be considered eccentric, not in flow with the culture, [and] so on. That's exactly what I want to be" (xi, 355).

So is Tom eccentric? Since the word, etymologically, means "out of center," or more loosely "off center," it obviously depends on what we consider to be the "center." If the center is the self, as in one being self-centered, obviously all Christians should actively seek to be eccentric. If the dominant fads and fashions of the present-day culture—that is, the spirit of the age, or the zeitgeist—are taken to be the center, Christians must choose between the timeless truths taught by Christ and His Church and the fashionable ideas of their own particular day. One who chooses the permanent things over the transient fashions will seem to be eccentric in the eyes of contemporary culture, and this is clearly the sort of eccentric that Tom says he wants to be. "To be a serious Catholic is going against the grain sometimes," he stresses. "That is just part of the price that you pay to do what you think is right." To put the matter in a nutshell, Tom appears to be eccentric because he is theocentric. He puts God at the center of his life.

This otherworldliness and theocentrism is clearly at the core of Tom's being as he approaches the sunset of his life and is indicative of the long way he has come since his days of incessant splurging and his life as a celebrity show-off. It also serves to show why he was unperturbed when several high-profile Catholics pulled out of the Legatus Summit in 2015 following pressure from the homosexual lobby. "I didn't feel alarmed when those people dropped out," Tom says. "I figured that it would be a good thing for Legatus. It just shows that Legatus matters."

In spite of some of its major speakers withdrawing at the last moment, the Summit was a huge success, with the second highest turnout ever. Tom is encouraged, though he is realistic enough to know that fair-weather Catholics, especially celebrities who are particularly vulnerable to political pressure, will not have the courage of their convictions in the face of the rising tide of secularist intolerance toward the Faith. "We're probably going to have a hard time getting celebrities featured in the future because they're vulnerable. We won't get people that are vulnerable because, you know, the enemies of the Church have us in their sights now." Tom is, however, not about to kowtow before the forces of the culture of death, responding to these latest political protests and threats with the same defiance that he had shown almost thirty years earlier when the

National Organization for Women protested against Domino's because of Tom's pro-life and antiabortion stance. On the contrary, he responded immediately to the latest threats by announcing that the following year's Summit, held in Orlando in January 2016, would be on the theme, "No More Comfortable Catholicism." "I selected this theme because I believe it is time for all faithful Catholics, and particularly our Legatus members, to live out our Faith with more conviction than ever before." Taking his lesson from history, Tom knew that saints, and those trying to be saints, do not abandon the good fight in times of rising persecution. On the contrary, it is at such times that saints come forward to bear witness to the Faith, mindful that another name for witness is "martyr."

As we move forward into troubling times, though certainly not more troubling than many other times the Church has seen, I wondered which part of Tom's legacy he thought would have the greatest impact on the culture over the next thirty years or so. At first, he was hesitant to answer. Then, falteringly, and perhaps reluctantly, he tried to play the prophet.

"The university has been a lot more difficult than I thought it was going to be, but if Ave Maria University can become a beacon for the other Catholic universities, for the two hundred and some Catholic universities, that could be really big. And then there is the law school which is training the future leaders of our country and the future lay leaders in the Church, so who knows where that could go? And it's so needed because there's twenty-seven Catholic law schools, and we're the only one that's genuinely

Catholic." He pauses, as if pondering some of the other initiatives that owe their existence or a good part of their success to his support. "I kind of realized one day when I was coming to work that right here in Ann Arbor, we've got one of the fastest growing religious orders in the country [the Dominican Sisters of Mary, Mother of the Eucharist]. We've got one of the top fifty Catholic high schools in the country in Fr. Gabriel Richard, and we've got one of the greatest parishes in the country, Christ the King, all right here in Ann Arbor. In addition, there is the radio station and the Thomas More Law Center."

All of the foregoing was impressive enough as a summary of the legacy of Thomas Stephen Monaghan but it was only a preamble. None of these entities would have as much impact, he believed, as Legatus. "I think the thing about Legatus is that it has the magic, if that's the right word, of the simplicity that Domino's had. The University is such a complex thing. There's more things that can go wrong. One component part of the University can make the rest of it go askew. Whereas the genius of Legatus is that it's a simple idea that's really working. There's no reason it can't grow exponentially, because it's a simple formula. It could spread around the world."

So much for Tom Monaghan's earthly legacy. What of his eternal destiny? Although the latter might be infinitely more important than the former, the two are intricately and inextricably connected. If Tom Monaghan gets to heaven, it will be the just and merciful reward for his life's labors. The life and the legacy will be judged as the road that he chose to take. If the life and legacy have led him and others closer to heaven, they will be seen ultimately as the path, lit by grace, that got him there. As he said at the conclusion to his autobiography, *Pizza Tiger*, published thirty years ago, getting to heaven is the ultimate purpose of his or anyone else's life. "My point, as I close this final chapter," he wrote, "is that I believe there's *something* in life that's a lot bigger and more important than Domino's. I have faith that God will help me find it, and that He'll show me the way to my ultimate goal, which is to go to heaven and take as many people as possible with me."

Asked many years later whether he still wanted to help people get to heaven, he answered as emphatically as ever: "Yes, what else is important? That is what education is about. That is what the university is about. That is what the nuns are about. That is what the schools are about. And you have people out there trying to stop me from doing it. I don't know if they don't understand what they are doing."

And yet, as James Leonard asked, what if there is no heaven and no hell? Would this have made Tom's life a waste of time? "That's Pascal's wager," Tom responded. "It's still the most enjoyable way to live, having that hope. It helps you be a better person, make a better world, just by believing in God, trying to obey his command- ments" (364). It was an apt riposte to the skepticism and cynicism of the world and its weariness. Why dice with death and the possibility of eternal damnation when you can live happier in this life by believing in God and perhaps live happily ever after in Heaven if the God you believe in really exists? Why would one wallow despairingly in the gutter, when one can be looking joyfully at the stars?

These are good questions for one lacking faith. But for one who has faith—or at least for one who has the Catholic faith, with its two thousand years of asking and answering the questions that the greatest minds have pondered—Pascal's wager is only one of the many rational signs that there is a God in heaven and that our only purpose in life is to join Him there. To know Him is to love Him, and to love Him is to find the peace that passes all understanding. Tom Monaghan is seeking to know and love God better in this world that he might be with Him forever in the next. This is the path of wisdom as it is ultimately the path of peace. Casting off the wealth and trappings of this world, the things that glitter in the gutter, he has raised his eyes to the heavens and has tried to help others do the same. This, when all is said and done, is his greatest legacy.

INDEX

Note: Page numbers with *n* indicate footnotes.

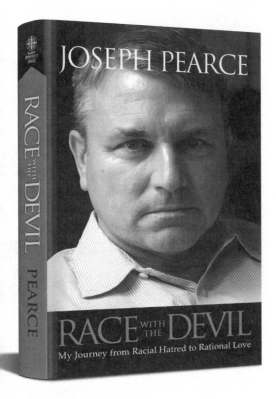

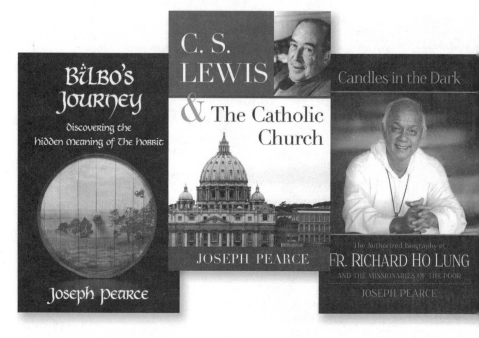

Discover the Christian meaning of *The Hobbit*

Bilbo's Journey Joseph Pearce

Go beyond the dragons, dwarves, and elves, and discover the surprisingly deep and Christian meaning of J.R.R. Tolkien's classic novel. Joseph Pearce takes you through the riveting tale, while uncovering the profound meaning that makes *The Hobbit* a truly timeless adventure. *978-1-61890-058-6 • Paperbound*

How Catholic was C.S. Lewis?

C.S. Lewis and the Catholic Church Joseph Pearce

C.S. Lewis is credited with bringing scores to the Catholic faith, yet never became Catholic himself. With expert scholarship, Joseph Pearce dives into this perplexing phenomenon, bringing answers to the surface. Contains a new Appendix of Catholics who credit Lewis for their conversion and a new introduction by Fr. Dwight Longenecker. *978-1-61890-230-6 • Paperbound*

The inspirational story of the "Mother Teresa of the Carribean"

Candles in the Dark Joseph Pearce

Learn the fascinating story of Fr. Richard Ho Lung, the founder of the Missionaries of the Poor, one of the world's fastest growing religious orders. Reminds us that God still works in the world. *978-1-61890-398-3 • Paperbound*

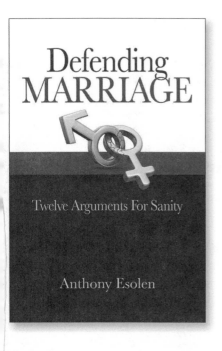
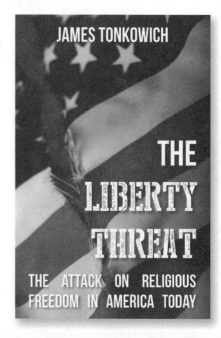

TAN·BOOKS

TAN Books is the Publisher You Can Trust With Your Faith.

TAN Books was founded in 1967 to preserve the spiritual, intellectual, and liturgical traditions of the Catholic Church. At a critical moment in history TAN kept alive the great classics of the Faith and drew many to the Church. In 2008 TAN was acquired by Saint Benedict Press. Today TAN continues to teach and defend the Faith to a new generation of readers.

TAN publishes more than 600 booklets, Bibles, and books. Popular subject areas include theology and doctrine, prayer and the supernatural, history, biography, and the lives of the saints. TAN's line of educational and homeschooling resources is featured at TANHomeschool.com.

TAN publishes under several imprints, including TAN, Neumann Press, ACS Books, and the Confraternity of the Precious Blood. Sister imprints include Saint Benedict Press, Catholic Courses, and Catholic Scripture Study.

For more information about TAN,
or to request a free catalog, visit
TANBooks.com

Or call us toll-free at
(800) 437-5876